Beyond the Handshake
Singapore's Foreign Service

Beyond the Handshake
Singapore's Foreign Service

editor

Lawrence Anderson
S. Rajaratnam School of International Studies, Singapore

NEW JERSEY · LONDON · SINGAPORE · BEIJING · SHANGHAI · HONG KONG · TAIPEI · CHENNAI · TOKYO

Published by

World Scientific Publishing Co. Pte. Ltd.

5 Toh Tuck Link, Singapore 596224

USA office: 27 Warren Street, Suite 401-402, Hackensack, NJ 07601

UK office: 57 Shelton Street, Covent Garden, London WC2H 9HE

National Library Board, Singapore Cataloguing in Publication Data
Name(s): Anderson, Lawrence, editor.
Title: Beyond the handshake : Singapore's foreign service / editor, Lawrence Anderson.
Description: Singapore : World Scientific Publishing Co. Pte. Ltd., [2022]
Identifier(s): ISBN 978-981-12-5860-2 (hardcover) | ISBN 978-981-12-6016-2 (paperback) |
    ISBN 978-981-12-5861-9 (ebook for institutions) |
    ISBN 978-981-12-5862-6 (ebook for individuals)
Subject(s): LCSH: Singapore--Foreign relations. | Diplomats--Singapore.
Classification: DDC 327.5957--dc23

British Library Cataloguing-in-Publication Data
A catalogue record for this book is available from the British Library.

Copyright © 2023 by S. Rajaratnam School of International Studies

All rights reserved.

For any available supplementary material, please visit
https://www.worldscientific.com/worldscibooks/10.1142/12900#t=suppl

Desk Editor: Lai Ann

Typeset by Stallion Press
Email: enquiries@stallionpress.com

Printed in Singapore

Foreword

As a small country, Singapore has no inherent strategic weight. Our ability to exercise influence comes from our global outlook, bold ideas and ability to deliver. Our Foreign Service and diplomats have to be exceptionally capable too.

When I was Prime Minister, my guiding principle on foreign policy was relevance. If we do not add value in a relationship, why would other leaders be interested in Singapore as a partner or even in our country's existence? How Singapore remained relevant to our neighbours, Asia and the rest of the world was always at the top of my mind.

Countries may have different interests and priorities, but they share similar goals in wanting to uplift the lives of their peoples. The key in advancing our foreign policy interests is finding the common goals embedded in our respective national agendas. Finding this sweet spot requires us to look at the world through the eyes of others, so that we can better understand their interests and concerns. Win-win collaborations are the best way to forge strong partnerships with other countries near and far, big and small.

But what if Singapore does not see eye to eye with other countries on some issues? Our priority then will be to advance Singapore's interests based on principles and the international rule of law. This similarly requires a good understanding of the perspectives of other countries.

All this calls for candour and trust not just in the overall bilateral relationship but also in personal interactions between leaders and between officials. Our officials should be sincere but not naïve, shrewd but not duplicitous. As Prime Minister, I focused on developing friendships and deepening trust with foreign leaders. It is easier to talk frankly and get things done when there is trust.

Our diplomats play a critical role in developing trust and friendship with other countries. Through their presence on the ground and the networks they build, they provide realistic assessments on how to pitch our initiatives and advance our interests. Innovative proposals such as the Asia-Europe Meeting (ASEM), Asia-Middle East Dialogue (AMED), Initiative for ASEAN Integration (IAI) and the Tianjin Eco-City were brought to life by our able and diligent diplomats. They took an activist approach and tirelessly engaged their foreign counterparts. They had the skills of persuasion and, if need be, cajoling.

I commend RSIS for publishing *Beyond the Handshake*, a collection of 21 essays detailing the personal accounts of some of our diplomats. They recount their experiences, successes, trials and tribulations in protecting and advancing Singapore's national interests. These lived experiences vividly flesh out the meaning of foreign policy and diplomacy. I have interacted with practically every one of the writers. They are sharp, respected and dedicated. They help Singapore punch above its weight.

The coming decade will be challenging. Geopolitical rivalries are threatening to divide the world, or worse, plunge it into conflict. Countries may be forced to take sides. The multilateral consensus on globalisation is fraying. The climate emergency poses an existential threat, especially to low-lying countries like Singapore. The COVID-19 pandemic has disrupted lives and changed our patterns of work and physical contacts.

For the Singapore torch to keep burning bright in this uncertain and turbulent world, we need more enterprising and dedicated diplomats. *Beyond the Handshake* is an inspiring read, and an especially useful launch pad for aspiring diplomats.

Goh Chok Tong
Emeritus Senior Minister
Prime Minister of Singapore (1990–2004)

Acknowledgements

This book has been a long-time coming. The brainchild of RSIS Executive Deputy Chairman Ong Keng Yong, he proposed the idea that retired senior officials from the Ministry of Foreign Affairs be approached to contribute essays on their experiences in foreign postings on how they had managed to advance Singapore's security and strategic interests and their assessments thereof.

Its editorial journey commenced with Ms. Viji Menon, who sadly passed away shortly after. Editorial duties then passed to Christopher Cheang who did much of the editing, clarification and corrections on many of the papers, as well as contributed an essay of his own. However, Christopher relinquished the project when he left RSIS last year. When Lawrence Anderson joined the think-tank as a Senior Fellow in November 2021, he was effectively tasked to marshal the book past the finish-line. He did this admirably, completing the editorial work, as well as contributing an essay and the Preface.

We would like to thank former Prime Minister Goh Chok Tong for his foreword to this book. We also wish to thank our contributors for sharing their tales, reflections and lessons learnt, as well as personal photographs of the events in which they had participated. Through their stories we hope a younger generation of Singaporeans will appreciate how our foreign policy was implemented to promote and protect Singapore's national interests.

Our appreciation also goes to our colleagues at RSIS, including Mr. Adrian Tan, Ms. Chew Peck Wan, Ms. Tan Ming Hui and Ms. Vanessa Tan Xin Hui for their help in the preparation of this book. A special mention to Professor Ang Cheng Guan for reading through the entire book and offering valuable and constructive advice. Finally, we wish to thank our editors and publishers, Chua Hong Koon and Lai Ann of World Scientific Publishing, for their efforts and support.

Ong Keng Yong
Lawrence Anderson
Singapore
5 May 2022

Preface

From having independence thrust upon this island in 1965, Singapore has experienced a meteoric rise to a modern and developed city-state. Singapore's current high-tech global city status is often attributed to the leadership and policies of its early leaders such as Lee Kuan Yew, S. Rajaratnam and Goh Keng Swee. Their contribution to the Singapore success story was vital. What is less known is the part played by its foreign policy and by the men and women who contributed to its implementation and success, as well as its missed opportunities.

Foreign policy is the conduct of a country's relations with other nations in the pursuit of its national interests. To a Southeast Asian island-nation 733 square kilometres in size, located at the southernmost tip of one of the world's strategic "choke points", the Strait of Malacca, bereft of any natural resources except for the resourcefulness of its people and whose high dependence on the international environment is reflected in its trade to gross domestic product (GDP) ratio[1], the importance to Singapore of conducting a sensible and successful foreign policy is self-evident.

Here then is a collection of essays telling the Singapore story from the foreign policy perspective. Three generations of Singapore's ambassadors and senior diplomats recount in their own words how they did their work, their experiences, achievements and shortcomings, as well as the difficulties that they encountered in promoting and safeguarding Singapore's strategic security and economic interests. Written in a readable style of personal chats and observations, it will bring back memories to older

---

[1] In 2020, Singapore's trade-to-GDP ratio was 320.56%, a 2.95% decline from 2019 due mainly to the COVID-19 pandemic.

Singaporeans who went through those tumultuous times and serve as a primer of useful lessons for Singapore, especially younger Singaporeans, as we go through an uncertain globalised world with its own set of unique challenges.

The Early Years

The story begins with some of the challenges facing us as a young nation. **V.K. Rajan** has pointed out that the top priority following independence was survival, and that meant securing international recognition of Singapore as a sovereign state by as many countries and as quickly as possible. To this, he added security, defence and economic construction, all of which had to be effectively dealt with and managed, not sequentially but simultaneously. And where did foreign policy fit into this? As **T. Jasudasen** has pertinently observed, the raison d'être of Singapore's diplomacy is to help secure and expand our political, economic and security space not just in Southeast Asia, but across the globe. The opportunities for expanding such space can spring forth through sheer serendipity, but more commonly they must be conjured up through careful identification and planning, with requisite nifty footwork to make it all happen.

Which brings us to the role of the Foreign Service and its officers (FSOs) or as **Bilahari Kausikan** has pithily titled his essay, "What Do Diplomats Do?" He rightly pointed out that diplomats utilise a range of techniques to advance or protect their country's interests, preferably by being pleasant, agreeable and tactful, but, if necessary, by any means that secured their objective. Since we are all different personalities, successful Foreign Services value diversity. He argued that the senior management and leaders must possess the self-confidence to trust their diplomats, allowing their officers the scope to be themselves, while maintaining the essential coherence and discipline that any organisation requires.

Lee Chiong Giam, who sadly is no longer with us, had emphasised from the start of his essay that Singapore diplomats, like others in our public or private sectors, must be diligent, able and honest in their collective tasks to promote and protect Singapore's national interests. He noted that as a young nation, Singapore was well served by capable personalities such as Tommy Koh, Chew Tai Soo, the late Kemal Siddique and others.

Subsequent generations of Singapore's FSOs would have a tough act to follow.

Baptism of Fire

The key foreign policy problem confronting Singapore and the region in the late 1970s right through the 1980s was Vietnam's invasion and occupation of Cambodia. It was this pressing issue that brought the Association of Southeast Asian Nations (ASEAN) together and occupied the energies of most FSOs based at the Ministry of Foreign Affairs (MFA) and at our missions abroad. Not surprising then that it forms snippets in the accounts of several contributors to this book. **Seetoh Hoy Cheng** has provided an interesting perspective of the conflict's early phase based on the meetings she attended of foreign dignitaries visiting Singapore. **Tan Seng Chye** covered it from the vantage point of his posting to Thailand, the frontline state, while **Mushahid Ali** was involved in different aspects through his postings in Kuala Lumpur, Jakarta and later as Ambassador to Phnom Penh in the late 1990s. **Bilahari Kausikan** cited an incident over Kampuchea's (as Cambodia was known at the time) representation at a Red Cross meeting to illustrate his thesis on what diplomats do, and he concluded his essay with a surreal anecdote when, much later as Permanent Representative to the United Nations (UN) in New York, he met one of Cambodia's deposed Royalist leaders.

ASEAN and Singapore

With the end of the Cold War in the early 1990s, Singapore's foreign policy priorities became more economic-centric, forging closer links to friendly states and all the major powers, as well as reaching out to the emerging markets of the former Soviet bloc and its allies in developing countries. Together with our ASEAN partners, we achieved the vision of ASEAN's founding fathers with the integration of Cambodia, Laos, Myanmar and Vietnam, and set milestones such as the ASEAN Free Trade Agreement (FTA), ASEAN Community and ASEAN Charter. Singapore took a proactive role in creating and shaping regional security institutions like the ASEAN Regional Forum (ARF); the ASEAN+3 process with

China, Japan and South Korea; the East Asia Summit (EAS); the Asia–Middle East Dialogue (AMED) and the Asia–Europe Meeting (ASEM).

Several contributors have dealt extensively with ASEAN matters at various times in their careers, but have not necessarily written about them in the book. However, **Ong Keng Yong** provided an insider perspective as the 11th Secretary-General of the organisation. His tenure from January 2003 till December 2007 covered the period when ASEAN was deeply involved with building upon the multiple regional security and economic platforms mentioned in the preceding paragraph with ASEAN in the driver's seat. Part of the problem was, and is, the belief among individual ASEAN members that they need not change or modify their national positions for the benefit and long-term well-being of ASEAN as a whole. Keng Yong noted rhetorically: Imagine the possibilities open to ASEAN acting in unison and tackling the challenges confronting them. His observations are even more valid today given the current uncertainties afflicting the region. **Barry Desker** has provided a balance between the varying strands of opinion on human rights to show how much ASEAN has progressed in this area.

Our Global Reach

Singapore's global reach can be gleaned from the dispatches and reports from its embassies in Asia, the United States (US), Europe, the Middle East, Africa and Latin America. Reading the disparate essays, one gets a good sense of life overseas as a diplomat promoting Singapore's interests. **Tan Chin Tiong** has written about his efforts in building on Singapore's excellent relations with Japan including helping to initiate state visits by Emperor Akihito and Empress Michiko in 2006 and later in 2009, the state visit to Japan by President S. R. Nathan and Mrs. Nathan. **R. Raj Kumar**, in his recounting of the Flor Contemplacion case in which a Filipino domestic helper in Singapore was found guilty of killing another Filipino maid and the four-year old son of the latter's employer and subsequently hanged after her trial, showed how bilateral quarrels can be managed successfully between two governments despite inflammatory public protests and statements. Similarly, **Robert Chua**, who suffered collateral damage in retaliation to the withdrawal of US diplomat Hank Hendrickson for having urged several Singapore lawyers to run against the ruling party in the

1988 elections, has given useful insights on how such expulsions can be handled sensibly and in a dignified manner in contrast to some high-profile cases involving other governments.[2]

Based on his experiences in Paris, **Tan York Chor** has highlighted the importance of being alert, persistent and proactive, and doing due diligence to seize opportunities to advance Singapore's interests, citing the examples of the Group of Twenty (G20) and leveraging on French culture. **T. Jasudasen** also wrote of his time as Ambassador in Paris, recounting not only successes in securing training facilities for the Republic of Singapore Air Force (RSAF) in Cazeux and persuading the renowned business school Institut Européen d'Administration des Affaires (INSEAD) to set up in Singapore, but also missed opportunities in not having two of the world's greatest museums mount regular exhibits in Singapore. **Christopher Cheang** was in Moscow when Russia and Singapore were strengthening bilateral relations, and he has provided an insider's take on dealing with the Russian bureaucracy in the post-Soviet era, as well as organised crime.

Turning to less familiar terrain, **Lawrence Anderson** spent six-and-a-half years in Saudi Arabia from 2013 to 2019 and had a first-hand view of the transformation taking place in the Kingdom. He has given a personal assessment on the trajectory and prospects of Saudi Arabia's political economy, society and religion; the country's foreign entanglements and insights into the successful workings of an embassy beyond the handshakes. **Tan Lian Choo** was responsible for setting up the Singapore Embassy in Brazil and has also outlined the importance of having a physical presence in the form of an embassy with staff on the ground. In writing on his experiences covering Rwanda, **Yatiman Yusof** has made useful insights from the perspective of a Non-Resident Ambassador. For instance, on how Singapore can serve as a model and inspiration to developing countries to succeed, even after experiencing a horrific civil war.

The Foreign Service in the 21st Century

Safeguarding Singapore's strategic security concerns and promoting our economic interests remain key responsibilities of the Foreign Service, but

---

[2] On a personal note, following Robert's departure, I was cross posted from our Permanent Mission in New York to take his place at our Embassy in Washington, D.C.

our national interest nowadays encompasses a wide range of diverse areas as well. With globalisation, the 2007–2009 financial crisis and the current COVID-19 pandemic, it is much about dealing with critical transboundary issues, promoting connectivity, sustaining regional and global supply chains, greater resilience of healthcare services, developing eco-friendly green and smart cities, and the judicious use of new technologies such as artificial intelligence (AI), big data and cybersecurity. Foreign policy involves looking indirectly at broader issues such as education, healthcare, job creation and the welfare of our people. As a corollary of this, a key task of Singapore Embassies overseas is to look after the safety and well-being of our citizens abroad.

Tackling these diverse responsibilities are reflected in several of the essays in this book. **Ajit Singh** covered the challenges in successfully navigating the labyrinth at central and local government levels doing business in India. **Bernard Baker** outlined how he helped to persuade the New Zealand government and unions to commence Air Services Agreement negotiations on 6th Freedom Rights. **Barry Desker** provided an insightful analysis of ASEAN's progress on human rights through the perspectives of the respective governments and civil society. **Tommy Koh** has written succinctly on his efforts at peacemaking both at home in Singapore and abroad in Malaysia, as well as his challenging role as the UN Secretary-General's Special Envoy to negotiate the withdrawal of Russia's military forces from the Baltic states. **Robert Chua** detailed his involvement in dealing with the devastation wrought by Cyclone Nargis in Myanmar, highlighting the need to coordinate efforts working with multiple Singapore agencies, international and non-governmental organisations, and both friendly governments and those suspicious of international intentions.

Postscript: What Makes Foreign Policy Work Beyond the Handshake

Foreign policy and diplomacy may have changed markedly from the time the contributors to this book began their careers in the Foreign Service. However, the fundamental aims of promoting and defending Singapore's national interests and many of the tools and techniques used to do so —

the grist of what needs to be done beyond the handshake — remain as relevant today as in the early years.

Virtually all the contributors to this book have provided valuable insights and advice on how a diplomat can operate effectively in varied environments, given differences in ethnicity, religion, culture and shared experiences. To the examples cited by different writers earlier, **A. Selverajah** has given his take on the responsibilities of a diplomat, the lifestyle and bearing, and the "essence of Singapore's proactive diplomacy". He also makes the pertinent point that the nature of the work in MFA HQ is so different from the responsibilities at post. **Lawrence Anderson** provided useful tips on information-gathering, the critical importance of building trust and cultivating the right contacts to give you access and a framework on how to make sound assessments. **Christopher Cheang** proffered advice on identifying the right sources, while **Tan Seng Chye** cited the example of his former boss to show how with trust comes great responsibility and unprecedented access to Thailand's policymaking circles. **Tan Chin Tiong**, **V.K. Rajan** and **Tan Lian Choo** have emphasised the importance of an embassy serving not just as a listening post and promoting relations with host governments but also protocol and liaison work, as well as increasingly having to look after overseas Singaporeans in distress. **Seetoh Hoy Cheng** has described the time when one of her officers had the difficult task of consoling loved ones of a deceased person.

The list will only grow longer once the pandemic is over and with more Singaporeans living, working and travelling abroad. The difference is that it will be to a younger generation of dedicated FSOs on whose shoulders lie the responsibilities of building upon the good work of their predecessors.

Lawrence Anderson
Singapore
15 February 2022

List of Contributors

A. SELVERAJAH served as Director-General for North America and Europe, and later Dean of the MFA Diplomatic Academy and Special Envoy for Arctic Affairs at MFA HQ.

His overseas assignments were Ambassador to the European Union, Belgium, Netherlands, Luxembourg and the Vatican (1999–2003); Ambassador to the Federal Republic of Germany with concurrent accreditation to Greece (2003–2008); Ambassador to the Republic of the Philippines (2008–2012); and Ambassador to the Republic of Turkey (2015–2019). He also served as a Non-Resident Ambassador to Denmark (2012–2015) and is currently Non-Resident Ambassador-designate to the Federal Democratic Republic of Ethiopia and the African Union.

During his 44-year career in the Singapore Foreign Service, **AJIT SINGH** served at Singapore Missions in the former Soviet Union, United States, Malaysia, Indonesia and India. In MFA HQ, he covered Singapore's bilateral relations with countries in Southeast Asia (Malaysia, Brunei, Vietnam, Cambodia and Laos), South Asia, Middle East, Latin America and Africa. Ajit Singh also held appointments dealing with ASEAN and international organisations, including the United Nations.

In a 37-year career in the Foreign Service since 1984, **LAWRENCE ANDERSON** served at the Singapore Permanent Mission to the United Nations in New York and Singapore Embassies in the United States and Thailand. He was appointed Ambassador to Cambodia (2004–2007), as well as Ambassador to Saudi Arabia and concurrently Ambassador to Bahrain (2013–2019).

Back home at the Ministry of Foreign Affairs, Lawrence at various times held appointments covering Singapore's bilateral relations with its Southeast Asian neighbours, regional policy and strategic security issues involving ASEAN and its relations with the Dialogue Partners, overseeing Singapore's technical assistance cooperation programmes as well as managed Singapore's relations with Australia, New Zealand, the South Pacific Islands, the European Union (EU) and other European countries. He retired from the Foreign Service in late 2021 after a secondment to the Asia–Europe Foundation. Lawrence is currently a Senior Fellow at the S. Rajaratnam School of International Studies (RSIS). He is also a Senior Fellow at the MFA Diplomatic Academy. He is Singapore's Representative on the Advisory Board of the ASEAN Institute for Peace and Reconciliation (ASEAN-IPR).

BERNARD BAKER was with the Ministry of Foreign Affairs from 1982 to 2019, apart from a 2-year stint with Singapore Airlines from 1990 to 1992, where he served in the airline's Public Affairs Department.

Bernard's postings abroad include assignments in New Zealand (twice), Canada, India and South Africa (twice). He served as High Commissioner to South Africa and concurrently Ambassador to Botswana, Zimbabwe, Lesotho, Swaziland and Namibia (2009–15), and High Commissioner to New Zealand (2015–19). Bernard also held several positions in MFA HQ beginning as Desk Officer for Eastern Europe and completed his stint as Director of Public Affairs (now Strategic Communications).

List of Contributors   xix

BILAHARI KAUSIKAN is currently Chairman of the Middle East Institute, an autonomous institute of the National University of Singapore. He has spent his entire career in the Ministry of Foreign Affairs. During his 37 years in the Ministry, he served in a variety of appointments at home and abroad, including as Ambassador to the Russian Federation, Permanent Representative to the UN in New York and as the Permanent Secretary to the Ministry. Raffles Institution, the University of Singapore and Columbia University in New York all attempted to educate him.

After graduation from the then University of Singapore, **CHRISTOPHER CHEANG** joined the Ministry of Foreign Affairs (MFA) in July 1980. He served in the Singapore embassies in Bonn, then capital of the Federal Republic of Germany (1983–1987); and in Moscow, Russia (1994–1997, 1999–2004 and 2006–2013); and the Singapore Consulate-General in San Francisco, United States (2013–2017).

As a career diplomat, **ROBERT H.K. CHUA** served as Singapore's Ambassador to the Republic of the Union of Myanmar from May 2006 to December 2017 and he was concurrently Dean of the Diplomatic Corps (2009–2017). He joined the Foreign Service in 1979. His previous postings were in the United States (First Secretary in Washington and Consul General in San Francisco), Japan (Counsellor in Tokyo), Philippines (Counsellor in Manila) and Vietnam (Consul General in Ho Chi Minh City). He served as the Senior ASEAN Member in the Myanmar–ASEAN–UN Tripartite Core Group in 2008 which was set up by the

ASEAN Foreign Ministers to facilitate the distribution of international humanitarian assistance to the victims of Cyclone Nargis in 2008. Prior to his retirement from the Ministry of Foreign Affairs, he served as Dean of the MFA Diplomatic Academy from January 2018 to May 2019.

Compared to his contemporaries in the Singapore Foreign Service who joined in 1970, **BARRY DESKER** had an unusual career. Barry was in Jakarta from 1976 to 1980, followed by New York from 1982 to 1984 and was Ambassador to Indonesia from 1986 to 1993. He spent the remainder of his 37-year career on postings in Singapore. Besides MFA HQ appointments, he served as the CEO, Trade Development Board; Director of the Institute of Defence and Strategic Studies; and founding Dean of the S. Rajaratnam School of International Studies. Following his retirement from the administrative service in 2007, he was appointed as the Non-Resident Ambassador to the Holy See and Spain. Barry was the Chair of the ASEAN Inter-Governmental Commission on Human Rights (AICHR) in 2018.

TOMMY KOH is Ambassador-at-Large at the Ministry of Foreign Affairs and Professor of Law at the National University of Singapore (NUS), as well as several other major appointments at the NUS. He is also the co-Chairman of the Asian Development Bank's Advisory Committee on Water and Sanitation.

He served as Singapore's Permanent Representative to the United Nations in New York, Ambassador to the United States, High Commissioner to Canada and Ambassador to Mexico. He was President of the Third UN Conference on the Law of the Sea. He was also Chairman of the Preparatory Committee and the Main Committee of the UN Conference on Environment and Development (Earth Summit). Professor Koh was the UN Secretary General's Special Envoy to Russia, Estonia, Latvia and

Lithuania. He was Singapore's Chief Negotiator in negotiating an agreement to establish diplomatic relations between Singapore and China. He was also Singapore's Chief Negotiator for the US–Singapore Free Trade Agreement. He acted as Singapore's agent in two legal disputes with Malaysia and chaired two dispute panels for the WTO. He is the co-Chairman of the China–Singapore Forum and the Japan–Singapore Symposium.

Professor Koh has received many awards from the governments of Singapore, Chile, Finland, France, Japan, Netherlands, Spain and the United States. He received the Champion of the Earth Award from UNEP and the inaugural President's Award for the Environment from Singapore. He was conferred with honorary doctoral degrees in law by Yale and Monash Universities. Harvard University conferred on him the Great Negotiator Award in 2014.

Born in 1941, the late **LEE CHIONG GIAM** joined the Civil Service in 1967 and held various appointments in the Civil Service including Deputy Secretary, Ministry of Foreign Affairs (1975–1982); Chief Executive Director, People's Association (1982–1999) and Non-Resident Ambassador to Papua New Guinea (1982–1999), Fiji (1997–2005), Pakistan (2005–2014) and Timor Leste (2005–2014). He retired in 2014 as the Ministry of Foreign Affairs' Senior Adviser. Sadly, Lee Chiong Giam passed away on 10 March 2021.

MUSHAHID ALI is a retired diplomat and former Senior Fellow at RSIS. He served in the Ministry of Foreign Affairs for 31 years, with overseas postings in Kuala Lumpur, Tokyo, London, Jakarta, Hong Kong, and in Riyadh and Phnom Penh as Head of Mission. At MFA headquarters, he served as Chief of Protocol in addition to holding appointments covering Singapore's bilateral relations with its Southeast Asian neighbours. He was also formerly a senior fellow in RSIS before retiring in 2020.

ONG KENG YONG is Executive Deputy Chairman of the S. Rajaratnam School of International Studies at the Nanyang Technological University in Singapore since 2014. Concurrently, he is Ambassador-at-Large at the Ministry of Foreign Affairs (MFA), non-resident High Commissioner to Pakistan and non-resident Ambassador to Iran. He also serves as Chairman of the Singapore International Foundation (SIF).

Keng Yong's ambassadorial postings include High Commissioner to India and concurrently Ambassador to Nepal (1996–1998), and High Commissioner to Malaysia (2011–2014). He was Secretary General of ASEAN, based in Jakarta, from January 2003 to January 2008.

Back in Singapore, apart from several assignments in MFA, Keng Yong was Press Secretary to then Prime Minister Goh Chok Tong (1998–2002). From 2008 to 2011, he served as Director of the Institute of Policy Studies (IPS) in the Lee Kuan Yew School of Public Policy at the National University of Singapore.

R. RAJ KUMAR joined the Singapore Ministry of Foreign Affairs in 1986. At Headquarters, he was deployed in the Southeast Asia Directorate (1986–1987 and 1991–1993) and as Deputy Director in the ASEAN Directorate (1996–1999). Raj Kumar served as First Secretary in the Singapore High Commission in Kuala Lumpur, Malaysia. Subsequently, he was appointed First Secretary and then Counsellor in the Singapore Embassy in Manila, the Philippines.

In 2000, Raj Kumar helped to set up the Singapore Consulate-General in San Francisco, and he was appointed its first Consul General. He also helped to set up the Singapore Consulate in Batam, Indonesia, in 2009 and was appointed as its first Consul General. Raj Kumar has also served as Acting High Commissioner at the Singapore High Commission in Pretoria, South Africa. Upon his return to Ministry

Headquarters in August 2013 he was appointed Deputy Chief of Protocol/Policy, Privileges and Immunities. In 2014, Raj Kumar was seconded to the Asia–Europe Foundation (ASEF) headquarters in Singapore as the Director of Public Affairs. He retired from service in 2016.

SEETOH HOY CHENG was appointed Ambassador to the Lao People's Democratic Republic in 2000. She was cross-posted to New Zealand in 2004 to assume the appointment of High Commissioner until 2009. She was concurrently accredited to Fiji from 2006 to 2009. Earlier, she had served as First Secretary in the Singapore Embassy in Washington D.C. from 1981 to 1984. She was Counsellor in the Singapore High Commission in London from 1989 to 1992. In Singapore, she was Director of Management and Personnel from 1994 to 1995 and Director of Administration from 1996 to 1997. She was Director, Policy, Planning and Analysis (Directorate IV), covering South Asia, Middle East, Africa and Latin America from 1997 to 2000.

T. JASUDASEN is a Singapore diplomat who retired from full-time diplomacy in 2014 after 37 years of government service. He is now actively engaged in the private sector apart from continuing with his diplomatic work as the Non-Resident Ambassador to Peru.

Jasudasen was previously Ambassador to France (1997–2004), Ambassador to Myanmar (2004–2006), High Commissioner to Malaysia (2006–2011), High Commissioner in London (2011–2014) and Non-Resident Ambassador to Ethiopia and the African Union (2015–2021).

Jasudasen has received several Singapore and foreign decorations in recognition of his services. The Singapore Government has honoured him with a Silver and Gold Public Administration Medal (PPA(P) and PBA(E), respectively). He has a Datoship (DSAP) from the HRH the Sultan of Pahang, Malaysia. He is an Officer of the "Legion D'Honneur" and a

Commandeur of the "Palmes Academic" from France. In the UK he is one of few Singaporeans to have received the "Freedom of the City of London".

TAN CHIN TIONG served in the Singapore Armed Forces from 1967 to 1982, retiring as Deputy Chief of General Staff. He was Permanent Secretary (Home Affairs) from 1982 to 1993, (Finance) from 1994 to 1995, (Information and the Arts) from 1995 to 1996 and (Foreign Affairs) from 1997 to 2004. He was Singapore's Ambassador to Japan from October 2004 to January 2012. He was Director, Institute of Southeast Asian Studies (ISEAS) from February 2012 to January 2018. He is currently Senior Adviser in the Institute.

He was awarded the Public Service Medal (Gold), the Public Service Medal (Military) (Gold), the Meritorious Medal and the Distinguished Service Order by the Singapore government. In 2017, the Japanese government conferred on him the Grand Cordon of the Order of the Paulownia Flowers.

A former award-winning journalist with *The Straits Times*, **TAN LIAN CHOO** joined the Singapore Ministry of Foreign Affairs in 1995, serving as the Ministry's first Director of Public Affairs, Spokesperson for the Ministry and Press Secretary to the Foreign Minister. Her overseas diplomatic assignments included being Singapore's Permanent Delegate to UNESCO in Paris (2007–2009), serving concurrently as Deputy Chief of Mission, Singapore Embassy in Paris (2006–2009). Lian Choo was appointed Head of Mission, Singapore Embassy in Brasilia, Brazil (2012–2015). She retired from the Singapore Foreign Service in 2015.

During a close to 39-year career in the Ministry of Foreign Affairs from 1967 to 2005, **TAN SENG CHYE** has served in Singapore's diplomatic missions in the UK, Thailand, Australia, Philippines, Laos and Vietnam. He was Ambassador to Thailand and concurrently Ambassador to Myanmar (1988–1990), High Commissioner to Australia and concurrently Ambassador to Fiji (1990–1993), Ambassador to the Philippines (1994–1995), Ambassador to Laos (1997–2000) and Ambassador to Vietnam (2002–2005).

In Singapore, at various times, he held several senior positions in the Ministry including Director, Political Affairs; Director, Policy, Planning & Analysis, Directorate I (Southeast Asia); Director, Technical Cooperation; and Director, Consular. After his retirement from MFA, Seng Chye joined the S. Rajaratnam School of International Studies (RSIS), NTU, as Senior Fellow from 2006–2020.

In his 39-year Public Service career, **TAN YORK CHOR** has served as Counsellor in the Singapore Embassy in Bangkok, Deputy High Commissioner in Canberra, Deputy Permanent Representative in the Singapore Permanent Mission to the UN in New York and concurrently Deputy High Commissioner to Canada. He was Permanent Representative to the UN and International Organisations in Geneva and to the International Atomic Energy Agency in Vienna, and Ambassador to France and to Portugal.

York Chor has also held appointments in the Ministry of Foreign Affairs at various times covering Singapore's bilateral relations with European countries and the European Union, and with various Southeast Asian countries. He is currently Senior Director and Senior Advisor in the Singapore Food Agency and its precursor (the Agri-Food and Veterinary Authority of Singapore).

V.K. RAJAN, a pioneer civil servant for more than 42 years, has held several positions in Singapore including Special Assistant to Director Manpower, Ministry of Defence and Private Secretary to the President. In the Ministry of Foreign Affairs, he was Assistant Director in charge of bilateral relations with Indonesia and later the Chief of Protocol.

He has served abroad at the Singapore High Commission to London, UK and the Singapore High Commission in Canberra, Australia, and as High Commissioner to New Zealand and Ambassador to Egypt, where he was concurrently accredited to Cyprus, Jordan, the United Arab Emirates (UAE) and Zimbabwe. At the time of writing, he is serving as an Adviser in the Bahrain Ministry of Foreign Affairs.

YATIMAN YUSOF was a teacher from 1965 to 1978. He became a journalist in 1978 and went on to become editor of *Berita Harian* and *Berita Minggu*. Elected as a Member of Parliament from 1984 to 2006, he was appointed as Parliamentary Secretary of the Ministry of Foreign Affairs in 1986 before becoming Senior Parliamentary Secretary in 1996, where he took on the appointment as Senior Parliamentary Secretary of the Ministry of Information, Communications and the Arts from 1997. He retired in May 2006. He was appointed as the Non-Resident High Commissioner to the Republic of Kenya (2009) and the first Non-Resident Ambassador to the Republic of Rwanda (October 2009).

Contents

Foreword	v
Acknowledgements	vii
Preface	ix
List of Contributors	xvii

THE EARLY YEARS — 1

Advancing Singapore's Security and Strategic Interests — 3
by V.K. Rajan

Seizing Strategic Opportunities for Singapore — the Quick, the Slow and the Missed — 11
by T. Jasudasen

What Do Diplomats Do? — 19
by Bilahari Kausikan

For Whom the Ambassadors Toil? — 27
by Lee Chiong Giam

BAPTISM OF FIRE — 33

A Lifetime Serving Singapore — 35
by Seetoh Hoy Cheng

Promoting Singapore's Political, Economic, Security and Strategic Interests in its Relations with Thailand and Australia — 41
by Tan Seng Chye

Observing Strategic and Security Issues — Diplomat on
   the Frontline 49
by Mushahid Ali

ASEAN AND SINGAPORE   57

Working at the ASEAN Level 59
by Ong Keng Yong

OUR GLOBAL REACH   67

Japan and Singapore: Growing Ties 69
by Tan Chin Tiong

A Diplomatic Crisis 79
by R. Raj Kumar

Reflections on My Career in the Foreign Service 83
by Robert Chua

Doing Due Diligence for Singapore's "Excellence" 91
by Tan York Chor

Working for Singapore's Strategic and Security Interests Abroad 99
by Christopher Cheang

The Kingdom and the Crown in the 21st Century 105
by Lawrence Anderson

Building Bridges to Brazil 113
by Tan Lian Choo

Rwanda — Mutual Cooperation from the Singapore Model 121
by Yatiman Yusof

THE FOREIGN SERVICE IN THE 21ST CENTURY — 127

Three Projects in India — Navigating the Labyrinth — 129
by Ajit Singh

Singapore–New Zealand Air Talks: Off to a Flying Start — 137
by Bernard Baker

Re-Examining the Human Rights Issue in ASEAN — 143
by Barry Desker

My Journey as a Peacemaker — 153
by Tommy Koh

POSTSCRIPT: WHAT MAKES FOREIGN POLICY WORK BEYOND THE HANDSHAKE — 157

A Career in Diplomacy — 159
by A. Selverajah

THE EARLY YEARS

Advancing Singapore's Security and Strategic Interests

by V.K. Rajan

My starting point is that Singapore was never meant to be an independent republic. The British ruled Singapore as a colony for 140 years from 1819 until self-government in 1959. Singapore depended on its survival as a centre for trade and commerce serving the hinterland of the Federation of Malaya (Malaysia since 1963). For various reasons, including economic and security, we sought to become part of Malaysia through a merger, but we did not seek independence and, above all, become a sovereign state.

Following Singapore's dramatic expulsion from Malaysia after the short-lived merger from 1963 to 1965, independence was thrust upon us without any warning or notice, effectively cutting us off from the hinterland — a development with very few parallels in history.

The number one priority on 9 August 1965 was survival and that meant international recognition of Singapore as a sovereign state by as many countries and as quickly as possible. Among other most important factors were security, defence and economic construction, which had to be effectively dealt with and managed, not sequentially but simultaneously.

I volunteered to serve overseas and was posted to our High Commission in London on 15 May 1966 as Attaché Administration. Apart from setting up the Mission our very small team went to work immediately in assisting our leaders, the late Prime Minister (PM) Lee

Kuan Yew, the late Dr. Goh Keng Swee and the late S. Rajaratnam, during their visits. Most importantly, our tasks were to:

- anchor Singapore in the British Commonwealth principally through the Commonwealth Prime Ministers' Meeting (as it was known then) and in collaboration with the Commonwealth Secretariat as a springboard to make a mark in the wider world;
- seek to delay for as long as possible the withdrawal of British forces from Singapore and other bases east of Suez to give us breathing space to make our own arrangements for our defence and security and also to deal with the consequential loss of jobs for our workers which contributed an estimated 20% of Singapore's gross domestic product (GDP) then; and
- make urgent arrangements to issue our own currency as quickly as possible by working with the Crown Agents and the Royal Mint.

There were other challenges as well. At that point in time, our Mission in London was probably the most active, stretched and stressed. We were new to diplomacy, and it was learning on-the-job. Unique problems required unique and sometimes unconventional responses and treatment. For example, we had to arrange for PM Lee and Dr. Goh to meet and speak to as many British members of parliament (MPs) as possible from both sides of the aisle during a weekend in Hyde Park Hotel in London. It did not give the MPs much time to travel from their country residences to London. As could be expected the MPs were not thrilled to forego their precious weekend with their families. Their body language showed. Yet, we managed to get a good number to turn up.

It was important for PM Lee to speak directly to the MPs to put our case to them. The success in getting the MPs under such circumstances also reflected the recognition and respect that PM Lee has earned so early in his political career, not just in the British establishment but in the wider society there as well. It was then also the height of the Vietnam War and PM Lee was sought after by the British media for interviews and often, we had to arrange them at short notice.

The late Prime Minister Harold Wilson's Labour Government was firm on a quick withdrawal but in a subsequent general election,

PM Wilson lost and the new Conservative Prime Minister, the late Edward Heath, helped us by agreeing to slightly delay the withdrawal. Given Britain's financial constraints then, that was as far as PM Heath could go. However, it gave us a bit of time to negotiate with Britain to agree to a modest package of measures for our defence and security, and to convert the military base to commercial enterprise, e.g., ship repairing and shipbuilding. We set up the Bases Economic Conversion Department. Thus, Sembawang Shipyard was inaugurated.

When PM Lee and other Singapore leaders were in London, it was of utmost importance for them to keep in touch with events and developments at home. In those days, the only means of doing so were the newspapers, both English and vernacular, and they had to be specially air-flown daily to reach London as quickly as possible. I would go to the airport in the very early hours of the morning to await the arrival of the BOAC[1] flight from Singapore. As there were no direct flights and with a few intermediate stops enroute, the flight would reach London some 30 hours later. I collected the newspapers and other dispatches as soon as they arrived and rushed them to PM Lee.

There was another important reason why time was of the essence. It was important for PM Lee to know quickly how his visits to London, his talks, meetings and negotiations with the British government and his attendance at Commonwealth Meetings were viewed and portrayed by pro-Communists and Communist leaders. It was no secret that the Communists and their fellow travellers, inspired by the ideology of and developments in China, had branded PM Lee and his colleagues as "imperialist lackeys", "running dogs of the British" and more. This was the ritual invective of the "Voice of Malayan Revolution" beamed from Beijing calling for the violent overthrow of the governments in Southeast Asia then. In the context of the time, I believed that the British also had a more than passing interest in how the deliberations in London were viewed in Singapore and by its neighbours.

My posting in London was very rewarding both in terms of the knowledge I had gained, the experience and the skills I had acquired and the satisfaction I had derived from my contribution to the success of the

---

[1] British Overseas Airways Corporation, the forerunner of British Airways.

Mission. With this background, I was tasked to organise the "Commonwealth Seminar on the Changing Patterns in the Conduct Foreign Policy" and the "Commonwealth Heads of Government Meeting" in Singapore in 1969 and 1971, respectively. These were the very early and important landmark events to seek a wider recognition and appreciation of Singapore's strategies concerning national defence, economic development, regional and global security, amongst others. A central plank in the strategy was a message to the world that, deprived as we were (and still are) of natural resources, Singapore did not seek aid from the world but sought trade and investments to build the nation.

Our consistent push was "seek trade, not aid". It was also a message to remind all our citizens that the world did not owe us a living. That strategy earned us respect and goodwill internationally, which were vital to attract much-needed foreign investments. This was in stark contrast to the policies of many other newly independent countries, which included seeking financial aid, war reparations and compensation for resources stolen by their former colonial masters. In a nutshell, our message to the world was that Singapore, as a "global city", would contribute a useful and constructive role in global governance.

Moving on, my job as Chief of Protocol gave me opportunities to build good relations with countries represented in Singapore. It was essential that their diplomatic representatives understood and appreciated the core underpinnings of our national strategy. It was important, therefore, to treat them well and be helpful to them. Their happy years and experience in Singapore would earn us much goodwill which would oil the wheels of diplomacy when our leaders and diplomats interacted with their counterparts abroad in a variety of settings. In training protocol officers and diplomats, both at home and abroad, I made the point that we should try to make them "our ambassadors" when they leave. As a corollary, transgressions of diplomats were dealt with in accordance with the relevant laws.

To achieve our security and strategic interests, I did not adopt a "one-size-fits-all" approach, or always a "standard operating procedure" in the countries where I served as Ambassador. Each country was different in many ways — history, geography, culture, politics, economic development, social make-up, the core elements in the bilateral relations and expectations, amongst others. Owing to space constraints, I list below just a few examples.

As High Commissioner to New Zealand (my first posting as Head of Mission) in 1990, I prioritised that, apart from managing the Mission well, I should concentrate on:

- New Zealand remaining engaged in our defence arrangements including the Five Power Defence Arrangements (FPDA). We could not and should not take their interests and commitments for granted, especially in the light of changing internal development dynamics. Besides the Department of Foreign Affairs and Trade, I also spent considerable time making my rounds in the Department of Defence and its related organisations exchanging views on topics of mutual interests and concerns. New Zealand had pulled out its small force stationed in Dieppe Barracks in Sembawang sometime in the late 1980s due to financial considerations. However, it was important for us that its commitment to the FPDA continued.
- addressing certain negative perceptions of Singapore in the wider society: that we were too authoritarian and were very sensitive to criticism and more. During a Q&A session following my keynote address at the University of Auckland on the 25th anniversary of ASEAN, a leading journalist questioned me on this. I was expecting this kind of questioning and thanked him for giving me the opportunity to put my case across. I referred him to a letter published in the *New Zealand Herald*. In it, a leader of a political party, a coalition partner in the government then, said that New Zealand was a holiday resort compared to Singapore which he likened to a prison camp. It was his reaction to a series of articles published in a Singapore tabloid by a female Singapore journalist after her tour of New Zealand. All the articles had noted the beauty of New Zealand, its friendly people and the pristine natural environment. However, one article also noted that there was a sizeable number of people on benefits (welfare) then, pointing out that in the 1950s, the records showed that the number of such people could be counted on the fingers of one hand. I then asked the large audience, "Now you tell me who is sensitive to criticism?"

I received loud and long applause. A few sought me out after the session to compliment me.
- promoting trade and investments to add substance and underpin the excellent political relations. The Government Investment Corporation (GIC) had invested in a few enterprises there. One such investment was the big supermarket chain named Countdown. Our Mission assisted in ways it could. I was also looking at the possibility of investments in their forestry, especially for the supply of timber and paper products. It did not materialise for a variety of reasons. Another area I considered was an investment in farms with a view to making New Zealand another alternative source of food supply for Singapore. However, the "tyranny of distance", amongst other problems, imposed an unsustainable high cost, especially transportation.

I had no reason to be dissatisfied with my performance. In a letter to introduce me to his Egyptian counterpart, Richard Nottage, the then Secretary of the New Zealand Foreign Ministry, noted, amongst other things, "New Zealand's loss is Egypt's gain." He noted that during my term I promoted a broad-based, deep and mutually beneficial bilateral relations through my proactive engagements of relevant actors — state and non-state, including political, business, security, academia, educational, civic and professional bodies, and thereby earned their respect and appreciation. Several of my lectures and keynote addresses were published in the print media and in relevant journals.

I was cross-posted from New Zealand to Egypt, with concurrent accreditations to the United Arab Emirates, Jordan, Cyprus and Zimbabwe. It was a different world but interesting, nevertheless. These countries were disparate groups and required different approaches. In general, however, my thrust was to deepen and broaden the bilateral relations to create a constituency of support for Singapore such as on issues affecting Singapore in the United Nations (UN) and other international organisations. We needed to be on their consciousness, and to achieve that aim, we had to find ways to be useful to them, forge suitable partnerships and thus add substance to the relations to sustain them over the long haul.

Egypt is an important, central and influential player not only in the Middle East but throughout the Arab world and beyond. Cairo still hosts the largest number of diplomatic missions, probably next to London. It is also an intellectual hub and a source of human resources (at all levels of administration) for much of the Arab world. It is the seat of many international organisations and representative offices, including the Arab League whose Secretary-General has almost always been an Egyptian.

In my view, there can be wars in the Middle East without Egyptian involvement, but there can be no durable peace without Egypt's participation. Egypt plays an active role in the UN and in other important international fora. Therefore, my mission was to build a broad-based constituency of support by engaging all relevant state and non-state actors to seek an understanding and appreciation of Singapore's strategic interests and policies, and our continuing contribution to global governance.

The modus operandi, apart from the usual cultivation of the official establishment, was a proactive engagement of academia, educational and think-tank institutions, diplomatic institutes, media, non-governmental organisations and other relevant professional organisations through keynote addresses, lectures, interviews, panel discussions, participation in international conferences and other interactions. Wide-ranging discussion topics included Singapore's public sector reforms including unique pioneering policies, e.g., Electronic Road Pricing; its development strategies; "Asia and the Gulf Cooperation: Prospects for Cooperation" (my address was published by the Emirates Centre for Strategic Studies and Research), Asian Financial Crisis and other relevant topics impacting the regional landscape and global governance.

Singapore had an on-going Technical Cooperation Programme with more than 100 countries from around the world. Singapore provides training in all fields of public administration and that was highly appreciated by recipient countries. (I was also a trainer in the Civil Service College which was one of the institutions involved in implementing the programme.)

In the other four countries to which I was concurrently accredited, my strategies and thrust were different based on the situation and local interests and expectations of those countries. Mainly, it was strengthening political relations by sharing our experience in good governance mostly through lectures, seminars to train their civil servants and participation in suitable events and engaging all relevant local actors across the spectrum. In short, make them feel that Singapore could contribute to their advancement. In Dubai, it was refreshingly different. At that time, Dubai had an active policy of "learning from Singapore" to adapt and adopt Singapore's development strategy and I assisted in ways I could.

I conclude this essay with a quote from my book *Serving Singapore: My Journey* (page 365):

> "I firmly believe that an ambassador should not become disheartened when every effort of his or hers does not succeed. I consider not trying as a bigger failure. Success and failure are two sides of the same coin. That is the nature of things."

Seizing Strategic Opportunities for Singapore — the Quick, the Slow and the Missed

by T. Jasudasen

This essay draws on a few stories from my tour of duty as Ambassador to France from 1997 to 2004.

By way of an introduction, it is important to stress that the raison d'être of Singapore's diplomacy is to help secure and expand our political, economic and security space across the globe. The opportunities for expanding our space sometimes appear through sheer serendipity, but much of the time they have to be created by careful identification, planning and the requisite nifty footwork to make it all happen. It is more often than not pure drudgery and sometimes can take years to achieve results. It is often about shooting at moving targets as priorities shift and change. Sometimes we just plain fail to bring home the goods because our competition did better and won.

All the stories that follow are about various Singapore government agencies working together as one (Ministry of Foreign Affairs (MFA) with Defence or Trade & Industry, or the Economic Development Board (EDB), or Culture & Arts), to seamlessly achieve our goals. This, I believe, is the real secret of Singapore's ability to punch above its weight.

The Quick Opportunity — the Republic of Singapore Air Force in Bordeaux, France

Maximising Singapore's limited land, sea and air space constraints is a well-told story. While innovative training solutions met most of our needs, right from the outset, the Republic of Singapore Air Force (RSAF) had few options but to seek flying space overseas. The search began a few years after our independence in 1965. Our first-generation pilots were trained in the United Kingdom (UK). Later, in the 1980s, for several years, the United States (US) Air Force allowed us to use Clark Airbase in the Philippines. However, in the 1990s, the Philippine government, in response to strong popular domestic sentiments, closed the US bases. Luckily for us, the US and Australia welcomed us to their home-based facilities for RSAF training.

Meanwhile, the search for a suitable jet training school continued. Informal soundings were made to a few countries and, where appropriate, followed up with formal requests. The British with whom we had defence treaty relations and a historically strong web of bilateral relations was a logical choice in Europe but for their own reasons appeared reluctant. Surprisingly the French, with whom our relations were quite insubstantial, were enthusiastic. At that time, hardly anyone spoke French in the Singapore establishment and even fewer in the Ministry of Defence (MINDEF). Our senior officers had been trained in Anglophone countries and had little understanding of French military doctrines or training processes. Therefore, it was a very courageous decision that the Singapore government took to seize the French opportunity in 1997.

The Stars were Aligned

Several factors converged in the late 1990s for Singapore to establish an RSAF training facility in France. We were the first foreign base in France after President Charles de Gaulle had removed the US North Atlantic Treaty Organization (NATO) bases in 1966 to 1967.

Firstly, the late President Jacques Chirac was the first French president with a deep knowledge of and extensive travels in Asia, especially Japan and China. Secondly, Singapore's late Prime Minister (PM) Lee Kuan Yew had built up a warm relationship with Chirac when the latter was still a junior mayor of Paris. Thirdly, with the end of the Cold War, Singapore and France were ready to think out of the box and explore new relationships. Fourthly, in Europe, defence budgets were being slashed because of the so-called "peace dividend" in the aftermath of the Cold War. Thus, cooperating with a foreign partner created a critical mass of activity and funding to justify maintaining more bases.

When the initial soundings between our defence officials were positive, we quickly moved to the next phase, namely identifying a suitable location for our flying school and negotiating a Status of Forces Agreement (SOFA).

The list of potential air force training bases was long. Undaunted, with then Deputy Prime Minister and Defence Minister Tony Tan and other senior defence officials, we criss-crossed the length and breadth of France via air, rail and road for on-site visits to consider the locational pros and cons. Cazeaux, located in the Bordeaux region, was my personal favourite. Apart from all the excellent military reasons for choosing it, Bordeaux was also my favourite wine region.

My role and that of my team of skilled diplomats was to support the Singapore defence experts with our language skills, figuring out local customs and negotiating styles and to help untangle cultural misunderstandings. For example, it was initially a huge shock for the conservative and rural French community surrounding the base. The idea that foreign pilots from the Far East, who spoke no French, were flying above their homes, schools and places of work, and Mon Dieu in American made planes, was beyond belief!

As I had studied in an elite French Grande Ecole, my French skills were good. In the build-up phase of our facility, my colleagues and I regularly visited the local mayors and municipal officials. We assured them that our pilots were extremely competent, that our planes were not prone to fall out of the sky and that they would be well-behaved and exemplary members of the local communities, where they would rent homes, raise their families and educate their children in the local schools.

Negotiating an SOFA is invariably one of the most challenging components in establishing an overseas military training facility. It lays out the rights and responsibilities and domestic laws that would apply to military personnel of both countries. As can be expected, there were ups and downs in the negotiations. However, as my classmates were sitting at the top of the defence establishment and at the Élysée Palace (President Chirac's Office), a discreet phone call was often all it took to unplug the bottlenecks and misinterpretations that inevitably surfaced from time to time. The SOFA was all signed and sealed before anyone expected it to be done.

Moving our Skyhawks to Cazeaux was an adventure in itself as they arrived by sea at Bordeaux port and were then transported by land, in escorted convoys to Cazeaux in the middle of the night to avoid inconvenience to road users. Roads were closed and some traffic and streets lights were dropped to allow the wide cargo to pass through.

In June 1998, the French held a formal welcoming ceremony to mark the commencement of the RSAF facility. And soon after we were ready to fly. It was a proud day for me as Guest-of-Honour at the first flight of our A4 Skyhawks in France, that were escorted by French Jaguar fighters. In 2018, we celebrated the Cazeaux detachment's 20th anniversary. To mark the occasion, Singapore was invited to participate in the French National Day celebrations to both fly and march with the Singapore flag. PM Lee Hsien Loong was an honoured guest at this parade in Paris.

Cazeaux was the first step in defence cooperation with France that helped build the bilateral trust and confidence that led to many other successful defence-related projects, for example the frigate-building programme for our Navy. The knock-on effect of high levels of bilateral comfort carried into various non-military areas of cooperation too. It was a win–win arrangement for both France and Singapore.

Taking the Institut Européen d'Administration des Affaires to Singapore

A key component of great global cities is the excellence of their educational institutions. To achieve our ambition to become one, we needed to build world-class educational and research institutions. Apart from growing them ourselves, that is organically, which was a slow and challenging process, we also identified several top schools and institutions around the world to invite to establish a programme in Singapore. France was home to Institut Européen d'Administration des Affaires (INSEAD), then and still continental Europe's most renowned business school, with a powerful international alumni network. A French school would also help diversify the Anglo-Saxon inclinations of preexisting institutions in Singapore.

EDB was tasked to lead this project and, where applicable, our embassies were an essential part of the wooing and lobbying of targeted institutions. Over time, EDB's dialogue with INSEAD bore fruit. While the Board of INSEAD was keen to accept our invitation to establish a co-equal branch in Singapore, the academic staff were reluctant to teach in Singapore. They had a caricatural and mistaken view that Singapore was a police state with neither academic nor political freedoms, as well as other reservations. When the Dean of the school shared with me some of the challenges he was facing, I volunteered to dine with small groups of potential academic staff to answer all their questions about Singapore. After several dinners, their understanding of Singapore grew, and resistance softened because I was brutally frank with them. I also drank lots of wine (it helped improve my fluency in French), smoked cigars and frequently swore in French which made me a fairly ordinary and human person and certainly not a right-wing fascist from a police state. Eventually, we had a good core of staff volunteers to teach in Singapore, but many swore not to stay beyond one semester. As it turned out, most of the staff found Singapore to be such an open, pleasant and intellectually stimulating experience that they renewed their stays several times over. And one professor never left at all! INSEAD's first Singapore Dean, Arnoud de Meyer, who had invested his heart and soul into the project, stayed on in Singapore. After his tenure as Dean, Arnoud was headhunted to become President of the Singapore Management University (SMU) and is today a prominent public intellectual in Singapore.

INSEAD Singapore was successful from the start. It gave comfort to other institutions of higher learning to follow in their footsteps to establish various programmes in Singapore. Today, every year, INSEAD draws some 200 top students from around the world (124 different countries at last count) and was the pioneer in helping in launching Singapore as a centre for learning in Asia.

European Union–Singapore Free Trade Agreement — A 20-year Pregnancy

At long last, and after I retired from the Civil Service in November 2019, the much-awaited European Union (EU)–Singapore Free Trade Agreement (FTA) came into force. It was much awaited because not long after I landed in Paris in 1997, then EU Trade Commissioner designate Pascal Lamy, a senior French civil servant, and then Ministry of Trade and Industry (MTI) Minister George Yeo met and agreed that it was opportune to soften the ground in order to prepare to formally negotiate an Association of Southeast Asian Nations (ASEAN)–EU FTA. In 1999, soon after Lamy was officially installed as EU Trade Commissioner, my instructions were to help raise support for the FTA idea from the French business community which was only partially sympathetic to trade liberalisation. Week after week, for more than a year, I called upon dozens upon dozens of business organisations in France to lobby them on the benefits of an FTA. The farmers' concerns were different from those of bankers, to those of traders, or to those of investors. I was not alone in this exercise. This was a whole-of-government effort and all our ambassadors in the EU member states embarked on this exercise: to plant a radical seed on infertile ground.

Unfortunately, though France was ready to move forward, many members of the EU were not ready and vetoed the project, allegedly in protest against Myanmar's political and human rights situation. To put it mildly, I was shattered that more than a year's effort had come to naught. The only consolation was the strong personal and institutional relationships built with many political, business and industry leaders. Later, when we launched other trade and investment initiatives, we had a ready-made pool of "Friends of Singapore" to support and guide us along.

All was however not lost. Singapore not surprisingly had a Plan B. We pushed for and succeeded in getting the EU to agree in principle to negotiate an EU–Singapore FTA that would serve as the model and pathfinder for an ASEAN-wide FTA when the time was right. While this idea had support at the Trade Commissioner level, the Singapore government next began a multi-year, multi-pronged process of active lobbying and visits to various EU regions to help construct an EU consensus among 25 member states. In France, I was able to activate our informal "Friends of Singapore" group to support this process of consensus-building. Elsewhere, it was a long and laborious process, often frustrating, and beset with many obstacles. In a nutshell, this was an exercise in herding 25 countries. While one member state might agree, two others would express fresh concerns. When you count the time costs of this exercise over the years, it would amount to many millions of dollars. As PM Lee Hsien Loong correctly noted in his Facebook account, the EU–Singapore FTA took a decade to negotiate. I think he was far too kind to our good friends in EU. The work on the entire process began much earlier. This was a 20-year long project!

The Missed Opportunities

It would be dishonest to claim that our diplomatic outreach to achieve national goals is a straight-line journey of unmitigated successes. Truth be told, the journey is strewn with outright failures due to superior competitors or because we misread the challenge or because of our own policy reverses even after much groundwork had been completed. Below I have one example of a Singapore policy change that led to others seizing what was in our bag.

Singapore's ambassadors often double or triple-hat, that is assume two or more Ambassadorial appointments, due to manpower and financial constraints. In Paris, I had the dubious honour of quadruple-hatting as Ambassador to France, Spain, Portugal and Israel. I was thus at the airport every month and very often more than once visiting various parts of my parish. On one such official visit to Bilbao in Spain with a ministerial delegation, our hosts invited us to the newly opened Guggenheim Museum of Modern Art. It was a stunning building that quickly achieved iconic status, apart from its superb collection of modern art. It was an international phenomenon — in today's speak, it has gone viral with Instagrammable architecture. My first thought was: why not in Singapore? Could we do something even better?

Happily, there was momentum and drive in Singapore for building our arts infrastructure and offering to our citizens and tourists. With the blessings of our senior arts officials, I reached out and cultivated good relations with the senior arts establishment of France especially with the Louvre Museum, the Centre Pompidou and the Museum for Asian Arts (Musee Guimet). The French officials were supportive of our ambition to upgrade our museums and they respected the professionalism and dedication of our museum personnel. They also dismissed the Guggenheim model as a cookie-cutter approach of the McDonald's variety. Instead, they wanted to work with a serious foreign partner who had a deep and long-term commitment to the advancement of the arts. During the early stages, Singapore officials were quite enthusiastic about exploring more and I was optimistic. However, our policies changed as we shifted gears, other domestic priorities loomed larger and the project was put into cold storage!

Several years later, in 2007, the Louvre Museum opened its first overseas branch in Abu Dhabi. I was happy for Abu Dhabi and the United Arab Emirates (a good friend of Singapore) but sad for Singapore. In 2019, the Centre Pompidou opened its first overseas extension in Shanghai. I was happy for Shanghai and China, another strong friend, but again sad that it wasn't in Singapore.

Can you imagine a Singapore with two of the world's greatest museums mounting regular exhibits? On the other hand, our pilots are still being trained in Cazeaux and INSEAD still draws the global brightest to Singapore and we have a robust FTA with the EU in these economically troubled times.

What Do Diplomats Do?

by Bilahari Kausikan

The general reader may find this an odd question. Foreign Service Officers (FSO) ought to know that the answer is far from straightforward.

Diplomats do diplomacy, but what is diplomacy? There are probably as many answers as there are diplomats as the rich diversity of experiences chronicled in this volume vividly illustrates.

Let me begin *my* answer by telling you a story.

A long, long time ago, in what seems a different universe, I joined a ministry that bears little resemblance to today's Ministry of Foreign Affairs (MFA). In late September 1981, barely four months after I joined, our then Permanent Secretary, the late S. R. Nathan, summoned Michael Cheok, who was then the Deputy Director in charge of international organizations, and me, the greenest of green desk officers.

On Christmas Day 1978, the Vietnamese had invaded Kampuchea (as Cambodia was then called). Hanoi overthrew the incumbent Khmer Rouge and installed a puppet regime under Heng Samrin.

Mr. Nathan told us that in little more than a week, the Red Cross would hold its 24th International Conference in Manila. For some reason — we never found out whether it was from sheer carelessness or some Machiavellian design — the Philippine Red Cross had invited the Heng Samrin Red Cross to represent Kampuchea. This would have given what the Association of Southeast Asian Nations (ASEAN) considered an illegitimate regime international recognition.

"Stop them attending," we were ordered.

"How?" we asked.

"You'll think of something" was the burden of Mr. Nathan's reply, adding, almost as an afterthought, that the head of the Philippine Red Cross was Imelda Marcos.

"Whatever happens the bilateral relationship has to be preserved and you are not to get our Embassy involved," he made clear.

It seemed that we were expendable. I commended my fate to whatever saints protect FSOs. Michael told me not to worry. I took him at his word.

In any case, there was no time for brooding. This was a non-governmental conference and diplomats were not invited. Michael and I hastily joined the Singapore Red Cross and off to Manila we flew.

We had only the sketchiest idea of how the international Red Cross was organised and operated. And in Manila, I soon learnt that much of what I thought we knew was incomplete or plain wrong. The Singapore Red Cross delegation was resentful at having their arms twisted to accept two shady characters. They wanted nothing to do with us and I do not blame them.

Neither was any other Red Cross delegation from any country helpful or even sympathetic. We were obviously not their type.

No other ASEAN country had bothered to send diplomats.

Michael and I were not exactly treated as unclean lepers, but it was close. The normal techniques of lobbying for support were obviously not going to work.

Desperate situations called for desperate measures. Michael requested a call on the President of the International Committee of the Red Cross, while I asked to meet the President of the Assembly of Red Cross and Red Crescent Societies.

These were very senior positions and there was no reason why either of these gentlemen should have agreed to meet obscure characters like us. But they were kind enough to do so. We repaid their kindness by threatening them.

Brushing aside their attempts to explain that the Red Cross was humanitarian and non-political — we already knew that — we demanded that the Heng Samrin Red Cross be disinvited. If they came to Manila, we would, regretfully but surely, wreck the conference.

In truth, we had absolutely no idea how to carry out the threat. Nobody would have lifted a finger to help us. But somehow, miraculously, it worked. The Heng Samrin Red Cross did not attend as planned.

I am still not sure why it worked. Perhaps it was our very incongruity amidst the *real* Red Cross that lent credibility to our threat and the senior leaders of the international Red Cross decided not to risk it. As likely, it was sheer dumb luck. Chance plays bigger a role in international affairs than some diplomats are willing to admit.

I tell this story for two reasons.

In common usage to be "diplomatic" is to be pleasant, agreeable or tactful. But diplomacy is fundamentally about advancing or protecting your country's interests, preferably by being pleasant, agreeable and tactful, but, if necessary, by any means that gets you what you want.

This is not something peculiar to Singapore. During the Second World War, the late Winston Churchill wanted the British Ambassador to Spain to press the late General Francisco Franco to release British pilots who had been shot down but escaped across France to Spain and were detained there. The Ambassador protested that to do so would ruin his relations with Franco. "Stuff your relations with Franco," Churchill is reported as having replied. "What do you think they are for!"

It is only the most shallow type of diplomat who thinks that his or her job is to be agreeable in all circumstances. Their careers normally do not progress very far because the strain of being constantly agreeable paralyses mental processes. Too many diplomats of this genre mistake form for substance. Some even think that being called "Excellency" actually makes them excellent. As the late Sir Harold Nicolson pointed out in his classic work entitled *Diplomacy*, some go quietly mad without anyone noticing.

Of course, this does not mean that you should go around poking people in the eye just to see what happens. You ought to know what happens if you poke someone in the eye and do it only if it serves some useful purpose. A good diplomat never insults anyone accidentally.

Successful diplomats deploy a range of techniques according to what is appropriate in a given set of circumstances. Of course, some personalities will naturally be better at some things than others. Successful foreign services therefore do not try to force their officers into a uniform mould shaped by the prejudices of their managements, but value diversity.

I do not mean diversity as understood by the politically correct. That kind of diversity is superficial, relatively straightforward to establish and generally does not take any organisation very far. Much more essential and difficult is maintaining the essential coherence and disciplines that any organisation requires, but nevertheless giving officers the scope to be themselves and deploy that deeper diversity to best effect.

Foreign service leaders must possess the self-confidence to trust their diplomats. Trust is the most important point of my Red Cross story.

Mr. Nathan trusted us to do what needed to be done and did so without fuss. He defined the goal and trusted us to figure out the means. I do not recall that he ever subsequently asked us how we did it or indulged in post-mortems to demonstrate how he would have done it better. It was sufficient that it was done.

I do not know if Mr. Nathan really expected us to succeed in blocking the Heng Samrin Red Cross. But that was not really germane. As I grew more experienced in the foreign service, I understood that all he expected was that we give our best. He won the trust and respect of his officers by respecting them. He sometimes lost his temper, but he did not demean us. He took responsibility for our failures. That left us with the confidence to focus on the job at hand.

This is crucial because diplomacy is never without some degree of risk. Diplomacy is almost always conducted in conditions where information is incomplete and events in flux, but where the imperative to act is immediate. Diplomats are sentient beings acting and reacting with other sentient beings. The very effort to understand something — just asking a question, for example — may well change the behaviour or situation you seek to understand in unforeseeable ways. Sometimes you will fail. International relations is a complex system of unpredictable feedback loops.

I don't want to push the point too far. Not everything is unpredictable. Some — perhaps even most — parameters will be known and will be relatively stable. But risk is nevertheless inherent in diplomacy, and some things will, despite all our best efforts, fail or have unexpected consequences.

In these conditions, unless a diplomat trusts his superiors not to throw him or her under the bus when things do not go as planned, the all too, too human response is to do nothing, or to passively await instructions, or to swaddle oneself in the anodyne: in short, to protect one's rear rather than try to do anything useful. Trying to avoid all risk courts irrelevance which is the biggest risk of all to small states.

We should not forget that if complexity creates risk, it also promotes agency. The feedback loops of complex systems create continually shifting kaleidoscopes of new possibilities. There is always something useful that can be done, if only we have the wit to recognise it and the courage to seize the moment.

How do we judge what is an acceptable risk? The key word here is "judgement". All good diplomats I have met in any country have had two inter-related qualities in common: situational awareness and empathy.

Situational awareness is the ability to remain focused on the essential amidst the confusing swirl of events; seeing things holistically, in their proper context and beyond the immediate. Situational awareness depends on empathy. Empathy is not to be understood as warm and fuzzy feelings, but as the capacity to put yourself in someone else's shoes and see the world through someone else's eyes. That is why the egotistical and the narcissistic are never good diplomats.

Diplomatic judgement — diplomatic instincts — rest on these two inter-related qualities. In essence, they involve understanding that the world is driven by multiple logics, not all of which will be mutually compatible. The role of the diplomat is to understand other logics in order to navigate through them, or try to reconcile them, or if that is not possible, to minimise the friction between them, and ultimately to manipulate them in order to achieve our own ends.

The selection of upper echelons of our public service is generally based on a diametrically opposed idea: that there is only one logic applicable across all domains and therefore if an individual has succeeded in one ministry, he is fit to lead any ministry. This is to my mind simply not true. Horrible examples easily spring to mind.

There are, of course, always exceptions. I think all FSOs of a certain vintage would agree with me that Tan Chin Tiong and Peter Ho who came to MFA from other ministries were outstanding Permanent Secretaries who brought MFA to new heights. But the point is that they were *exceptional*.

For those of us — the vast majority — who are not exceptional, diplomatic instinct is the name we give to the accumulation of experience and reflection upon it: our own direct experiences and, perhaps more importantly since any individual's experiences are necessarily limited in time and space, the tacit knowledge we can derive from the experiences of others. That tacit dimension of knowledge cannot be taught; it can only be acquired, almost by osmosis. And it goes without saying that to learn from the experiences of other FSOs, you have to first trust and respect them.

For FSOs of my generation, our most important experiences centred around the Cambodian issue. Almost all of us, no matter which desk we were on or where we were posted, in one way or another worked on that issue. For a decade, it intersected almost every dimension of Singapore's foreign policy. Dealing with Cambodia was where we learnt our trade, and often we learnt it by making it up as we went along.

I started this essay with an anecdote from the beginning of the Cambodian saga. Concluding with another anecdote from its end might interest younger readers.

An agreement on Cambodia was reached in Paris in 1991. The Vietnamese withdrew and United Nations (UN)-supervised elections were held in 1992. A new chapter began for Cambodia.

But only five years after the 1992 election, in 1997 its results were voided by a coup that put in place largely the same government that the Vietnamese had installed at the beginning of the 1980s. Subsequent elections, which have been criticised by some countries, have in essence served only to validate the results of that 1997 coup.

To me, the only really surprising thing about the 1997 coup was that it took so long to happen. Almost a decade of working with the Coalition Government of Democratic Kampuchea (CGDK), as we termed those resisting Vietnamese occupation, had led me to conclude that the most competent part of the CGDK was the Khmer Rouge (KR). Officials of its non-communist components, FUNCINPEC (the French acronym for the National United Front for an Independent, Neutral, Peaceful and Cooperative Cambodia, a royalist party) and the Khmer People's National Liberation Front (KPNLF), were, with very few exceptions, personally likeable but politically effete, ineffectual and incompetent, with a mentality of entitled dependency. In the diplomatic contests at the UN and in the

Non-Aligned Movement, the only party in the CGDK that really could be relied on to deliver what they said they would do was the KR.

Whatever else you may accuse him of, you cannot call Prime Minister Hun Sen effete or ineffectual or incompetent. You may not approve of his methods of governance, but it is hard to deny that Cambodia is now in a better condition than in 1997. I for one would not be confident that Cambodia would be in the same condition if FUNCINPEC or KPNLF leaders or their ilk were running the country.

In 1997, I was Singapore's Permanent Representative to the UN in New York. After the coup, the late Prince Norodom Ranariddh, leader of FUNCINPEC and son of the late Prince (later King) Norodom Sihanouk, turned up in New York and sent word that he wanted to see me. As I entered his suite in a five-star hotel, Ranariddh greeted me in his high-pitched voice that was a caricature of his father's voice, with these words: "Bilahari, the struggle begins again."

What he said is seared in my memory. I could hardly believe my ears. I told him, as politely as possible, that he had been given his chance and this time the struggle, if there was to be one, was his struggle, not Singapore's struggle or ASEAN's struggle. He looked rather bemused and I wasn't sure he registered the point. Then, strangely, he said, "A cat is a cat and a coup is a coup." He seemed to savor the phrase, repeating it several times as if rehearsing a speech. As quickly as I decently could, I left.

For Whom the Ambassadors Toil?

by Lee Chiong Giam

Some people believe that diplomats are men in lounge suits and women in glittering gowns whose jobs seem to be just savouring fine wines, aged whiskies and succulent Kobe beef at receptions and dinners. Hence, in fairness to the maligned diplomats, I have amended the Arab pun about them to read: "A camel can drink for days without working. An ambassador can work for days without drinking."

Indeed, Singapore diplomats, like others in our public or private sectors, must be diligent, able and honest in their collective tasks to promote and protect Singapore's national interests. In a nutshell, our national interests are security, racial harmony, social cohesion and economic growth. Our foreign policy must continue to be the projection of these national interests.

Our diplomats' tasks have been made easier only because our first Prime Minister (PM), the late Lee Kuan Yew, and his successors have always set clear and achievable goals for Singapore's security, domestic harmony and prosperity. The Ministry of Foreign Affairs has also been blessed with excellent ministers, permanent secretaries, ambassadors and support staff.

We are still a relatively young nation. We should continue to be modest about our many achievements and whenever we can, we should also help other countries mainly through our Singapore Cooperation Programme. I will now pick some examples of our diplomatic achievements.

Law of the Sea Convention

I regard Professor Tommy Koh as one of Singapore's national treasures. He is exceptionally brilliant, eloquent, humble, multi-dexterous and patriotic. Professor Koh has served Singapore excellently in varied national posts such as Chairman of the National Arts Council, Singapore Ambassador to Washington and the United Nations (UN), and Dean of the Law Faculty of the National University of Singapore.

Among Professor Koh's greatest achievements were the agreements that were concluded when he was President of the Third UN Conference on the Law of the Sea in 1981. The Law of the Sea Convention sets the rules on territorial waters, international waters, archipelagic seas, straits and other related issues. These law-and-order matters are very important and beneficial to us as Singapore is one of the world's busiest ports. His success in shepherding the agreements has benefitted not only Singapore, but the world.

Diplomatic Relations with China

In 1972, China was admitted into the UN and as a permanent member of the Security Council. For good reasons, Singapore had decided to establish diplomatic relations with China, only after Indonesia. Meanwhile, Singapore would develop its bilateral ties with China. Hence, on 7 October 1974, the late Foreign Minister Mr. S. Rajaratnam hosted a dinner in New York for the late Chinese Deputy Foreign Minister Mr. Qiao Guanhua. Professor Koh and I were at this dinner. It was at the dinner that both countries agreed to begin with the exchanges of visits by their leaders to promote bilateral ties and establish diplomatic relations at the right time. And so, Foreign Minister Rajaratnam made the first Singapore Ministerial visit to China. In May 1976, PM Lee embarked on the historic visit to China during which he met the late Mao Zedong. It was Mao's penultimate meeting with the Head of Government before he died on 9 September 1976.

Since 1977, I have visited China many times. In September 1977, I went to China under an open cover as an Advisor with the Singapore Rubber Association. In 1980, I led a delegation to decide on the details of establishing a Commercial Representative Office in our respective countries in 1981. In 1990, I was with Professor Koh's delegation to finalise the terms to establish diplomatic relations on 3 October 1990.

Enhancing Diplomatic Weight

As Singapore is a small country, we need to be strong, successful and helpful so that other countries will respect us and want to deal with us. Success will help Singapore enhance its political, economic and diplomatic weight.

One way is to form, initiate or join an organisation or group of countries that share similar interests. The UN and the Association of Southeast Asian Nations (ASEAN) are the two most important organisations we have joined.

When Ambassador Chew Tai Soo was our Permanent Representative to the UN, he founded and chaired the Forum of Small States for countries with a population of less than 10 million people. Under Ambassador Chew's leadership, the Forum was active in promoting the interests of Singapore and the other members.

Graduation and the Generalised System of Preferences

The late Ambassador Kemal Siddique, or as he preferred to be called by his nickname "Tony", was one of the most remarkable diplomats we have had. Effectively multi-lingual and multi-talented, Tony joined the Ministry of Foreign Affairs (MFA) in 1970 after he failed to get a ticket to contest for a seat in Parliament. What was Parliament's loss was a gain for MFA. Tony was not dashing or handsome, but he was very eloquent — he could talk until a migrating bird would land on his right palm. His other saving grace was that as he aged, he began to look like the Soviet Union's founding leader Vladimir Lenin.

Tony came to MFA at a time when Singapore was still enjoying the perks of free access and other trade concessions offered under the Generalised System of Preferences (GSP) by developed countries to help developing countries export their goods and services. As Singapore made rapid economic progress through very hard work, some quarters in developed countries were opposed to continue giving GSP concessions to us. Instead, they wanted to "graduate" Singapore from the GSP. Together with other ministries, MFA fought hard against our premature "graduation". We were aware that we would eventually lose the fight, as our economic development was faster than many countries. Hence, the collective task then was to do everything to delay graduation for as long as possible so that our economic foundations would be firmer and stronger when we had to compete in the international open market.

As a young Charge d'Affaires ad interim in Bonn, Tony did an excellent job in lobbying German leaders and officials to support our efforts. For example, when we heard that there was a move to stop or reduce the trade concessions for our export of electronic calculators to Europe, we alerted Tony and he went to town to stop it.

Non-Resident Ambassadors

In 1981, the late Australian Ambassador, Mr. Tom Critchley, called on PM Lee. During the meeting, Ambassador Critchley suggested that as a small country with limited manpower, Singapore could not afford to establish embassies in many countries. Hence, it should consider appointing roving ambassadors to some countries. The Roving Ambassador should visit his host country regularly to promote bilateral economic and other ties.

PM Lee agreed with Ambassador Critchley's suggestion and I was appointed as Singapore's first "Roving Ambassador" to Papua New Guinea (PNG) on 6 October 1982. The term "Roving Ambassador" was subsequently replaced by "Non-Resident Ambassador (NRA)". The term "Roving" seemed to suggest that the Ambassador was just "roving" or wandering aimlessly around.

Working as the Chief Executive Director of the People's Association for 17 years from 1982 to 1999, I also served concurrently as NRA to PNG during the same period. PNG, with a land area of 500,000 square miles, is the largest developing country in the South Pacific. It is endowed with abundant oil, gas and minerals. Its seas are teeming with fish such as tuna. Apart from direct shipping links, Air Niugini and Singapore Airlines also serviced each other's countries. Hence, with my appointment as NRA and the assistance of a young Singaporean Honorary Consul, Mr. Victor Yu who was based in Port Moresby, we were able to promote more trade and services between our two countries. The airlinks also facilitated the frequent visits of PNG leaders to Singapore. I have also served as NRA to Fiji (1997–1999), Pakistan (2005–2015) and Timor Leste (2005–2014).

The success of the NRA scheme of service encouraged Singapore to appoint NRAs to cover more than 40 countries. Singapore's system of appointing NRAs is a stringent but simple process. Only successful professionals, entrepreneurs, executives and civil servants are considered. The logic is that if they are so successful in their careers or businesses, they must already have the right mix of EQ and IQ to be instant ambassadors. Our past and present NRAs include former Permanent Secretary Herman Hochstadt; architect Tan Kah Hoe; the late Director of Trade Ridzwan Dzafir; entrepreneur Gopinath Pillai; former Members of Parliament Chandra Das, Yatiman Yusoff, Chay Wai Chuen and Zainal Abidin; and Singapore's first lady NRA Ms. Pang Cheng Lian.

The NRAs have done a great job in promoting bilateral ties with their host countries. They have also excelled in other diplomatic tasks such as lobbying for Singapore's candidates for important international posts such as the UN Security Council and the World Intellectual Property Organization. By the way, the appointment of NRAs is also a delight to our Treasury. Except for an annual honorarium of about S$5,000, they receive no salaries. To them, it is an honour to serve Singapore as its NRA.

Singapore's future diplomats must build on the success of our pioneering and current generations in their services to our country.

BAPTISM OF FIRE

A Lifetime Serving Singapore

by Seetoh Hoy Cheng

I entered service at the Ministry of Foreign Affairs (MFA) in mid-November 1974. My first three years were spent in MFA's Regional and Economic Division and Administration Division. In 1978, I joined the Political Division and assumed responsibility as the Desk Officer for our relations with Africa, South Asia, Middle East and Latin America.

Work in MFA Headquarters

One of my tasks was notetaker for Singapore's first and longest serving Foreign Minister, the late S. Rajaratnam, during his meetings with the ambassadors and foreign visitors from the countries under my purview. His meeting room had an aquarium in the wall that kept waiting guests occupied.

The 1970s were difficult times. South Vietnam and Cambodia fell to the communists in 1975. A few years later, Vietnam invaded Cambodia in December 1978. At the beginning of 1979, China invaded Vietnam to teach the latter a lesson. Cambodia was then a de facto ally of China. The Soviet Union invaded Afghanistan in December 1979. Ambassadors called on Minister Rajaratnam and the late First Permanent Secretary (1PS) S. R. Nathan separately for their assessments of the situation in Afghanistan and Cambodia. China withdrew its forces from Vietnam a month later in March 1979. I was the notetaker at those meetings even when the Ambassador was from the United States (US) or Australia since they discussed the situation in Afghanistan which was under my purview. The late US Ambassador Richard Kniep would smile and say, "Sorry to give you so much work."

Sometimes when an ambassador called on 1PS to discuss Vietnam's invasion of Cambodia or the Chinese invasion of Vietnam, I would be the notetaker. 1PS was very kind. He told me that if he asked a question on the troop strength, it meant he wanted the figure recorded. He wanted detailed notes. He also sent me to the Prime Minister's Office (PMO) to take notes of meetings between the Prime Minister (PM) and foreign leaders of countries under my purview. Besides the curriculum vitae (CV) of the foreign visitor, the CV of the MFA notetaker had also to be sent to PMO before the meeting.

Vietnam invaded Cambodia in 1978 purportedly to help the people remove a genocidal regime. The Soviet Union invaded Afghanistan in 1979, claiming that the late Afghan President Hafizullah Amin was a "traitor" and a "CIA agent" as justification for the military invasion. On principle, as a small nation, we cannot accept that any country could invade a neighbouring country because it disagreed with its neighbour's policy.

Minister Rajaratnam, in his calm manner, thought of ways to garner international support to oppose such military invasions. Given his previous experience in the press, he had a booklet "From Phnom to Kabul" produced in 1980. This 52-page booklet was sent to all the Foreign Ministers with a covering letter from him. The booklet explained the problem and the consequences of Vietnam's invasion of Cambodia, known then as Democratic Kampuchea (DK). Singapore advocated the continued seating of DK at the United Nations (UN) because of the future implications for all small states in condoning or approving the overthrow of even a hateful government by a foreign army. Approval of such an overthrow would be a radical departure from the principle that the overthrow of an unsatisfactory government is a matter for the citizens of the country concerned.

For several years, the Singapore delegation to the annual UN General Assembly (UNGA) lobbied strongly for support for the DK Resolution. I was in the Singapore delegation to the 1986 UNGA. If the foreign delegate agreed to give his support for the Resolution, we had to ensure that he would be present to vote on it. Hence, we would look for the delegates to take their seats before voting began. Fortunately, we usually received more votes of support than the previous year.

In October 1980, I was a member of PM's delegation to the Commonwealth Heads of Government Regional Meeting (CHOGRM) in

New Delhi.[1] The Commonwealth and the Non-Aligned Movement also came under my purview. The Director of our Political Division and I arrived in New Delhi a day before the late PM Lee Kuan Yew. One of the problems we had to resolve was to keep the telephone from ringing in PM's room. It was not to ring at all. We spent a great deal of time getting the hotel to do this. Everything was lost in interpretation.

Mr. Rajaratnam's successor, Mr. S. Dhanabalan, then Principal Private Secretary to PM, Press Secretary to PM, Director of Internal Security and the Desk Officer for South Asia accompanied PM and Mrs. Lee on this trip. I accompanied Minister Dhanabalan to his meeting with the Indian Minister for External Affairs. At the request of PM's aide, I also accompanied Mrs. Lee to an event organised by the Indian government. At this Conference, Singapore and India had differences over the latter's support for Vietnam on Cambodia. PM Lee and the late PM Indira Gandhi had a four-eye meeting. Singapore also had differences with Australia. Nevertheless, the late Australian PM Malcolm Fraser offered PM a flight home to Singapore on his aircraft. While waiting for PM Lee to come in for the press conference, his Press Secretary asked me to help to request the people in the room to refrain from smoking during the press conference in the New Delhi hotel. Fortunately, the people cooperated. Foreign Service Officers (FSO) do everything to make everything run smoothly.

Work Abroad

FSOs provide consular services to Singaporeans. I started my tour of duty in London as Acting High Commissioner for two months in 1989. I met many Singaporeans studying or working in the United Kingdom. Less than a year in London, one of my former bosses called me to find a Singapore nurse to accompany his aunt back to Singapore. His aunt had suffered a stroke. The family would pay the return passage to Singapore, business class to Singapore and economy fare back to London for the nurse. I called my Singapore contact, and a Singapore nurse was found immediately.

---

[1] This biennial meeting which alternated with the biennial Commonwealth Heads of Government Meeting (CHOGM) subsequently ceased.

One day, a young consular officer told me that he was disturbed by the loud scream of the parent of a deceased Singaporean after his call to the latter. I advised him never to directly inform the parent that his or her child had passed away. One should speak to the sibling of the deceased as that person would know how best to break the news to the parent. It would be better to inform MFA Headquarters so that they could break the news to the next of kin.

In early 2000, I was appointed Ambassador to Lao People's Democratic Republic (Lao PDR), a landlocked country. Given its geographical location and limited air links, trade between the Singapore and Lao PDR was and is low. SilkAir ceased operating to Vientiane during the 1998 Asian Financial Crisis. In 2000, I could not persuade Singapore Airlines (SIA) to resume flights even after the Lao Minister told me that sixth freedom rights would be given.[2] At that time, there was no passenger or cargo load for SIA.

Singapore has offered many training courses to Lao officials and arranged study visits for the provincial governors and other senior officials in the central committee of the ruling party. Our Agri-Food and Veterinary Authority of Singapore (AVA) developed a red tilapia fish farm in Laos in 2001. It also provided the fry. The Lao–Singapore Training Institute was established in Vientiane in 2002 so that more Lao officials could be trained in English language; such courses were important to Lao officials and politicians, especially when they attended international meetings where there was no simultaneous interpretation.

I lobbied Lao officials for support for UN resolutions of importance to Singapore. Lao PDR did not support Singapore on the UN High Commission for Human Rights Resolution on capital punishment. Capital punishment was in force in Laos. My first task was to persuade Lao Foreign Ministry officials to support Singapore on the UN resolution on capital punishment. I received that support from Lao officials for four consecutive years. Lao PDR did not have an office in Geneva. A delegation from Vientiane attended the Assembly in April in Geneva every year.

Singapore wanted to host the Regional Cooperation Agreement on Combatting Piracy and Armed Robbery (RECAAP) centre. As a maritime

---

[2] Sixth freedom rights refer to certain privileges of air services, in this case allowing SIA to operate in Laos and carry passengers/cargo to two other states.

nation, RECAAP is important for Singapore. I spoke to Lao officials to seek their support. One official told me that Malaysia and Indonesia had also sought Lao's support. I urged him to look at the merits of Singapore's location and Singapore–Lao relations. Eventually a senior official agreed to support Singapore. I told him that the Lao delegate must speak in support of Singapore's bid at the conference, and that I had every confidence he would do it. He said that his delegate would not know what to say. I assured the Lao official that I would ask the Singapore delegation to help the Lao delegate with the statement. Notwithstanding the fact that we were competing with our immediate neighbours, we always help others with their statements when English is not their first language. We won the bid.

I also sought to gain Lao's support for Singapore's bid for a seat on the expanded International Civil Aviation Organization (ICAO) council. Then Singapore informed me that Laos could not vote because it had not ratified the amendment to Article 50(a) of ICAO's Chicago Convention. I went to see the President of the Lao Parliament, a politburo member. He told me that Parliament would not be meeting for several months. I informed the Vice Minister for Foreign Affairs of my problem. He said that the Deputy Prime Minister and Foreign Minister could give me the instrument of ratification in a few days. A week after collecting the document, I went to remind the International Organisations Director to vote in support of Singapore at the ICAO Assembly. He told me that they did not have the human and financial resources to send anyone from Vientiane to the Assembly in Montreal. I suggested that an officer from the Lao UN office in New York could be sent to Montreal. A few days later, he told me that a Lao delegate from New York would attend the ICAO Assembly. Singapore was elected to the ICAO in March 2003.

In early 2004, I was assigned as High Commissioner to New Zealand and concurrently accredited to the Republic of Fiji Islands in 2006. I was appointed Special Envoy in 2007 to Cook Islands, Fiji, Kiribati, Samoa and Tonga to lobby their support for Singapore's candidacy for a seat each in the ICAO Council and the International Maritime Organisation (IMO) Council. I was accompanied by a director and a manager from the Civil Aviation Authority of Singapore (CAAS). I met the officials, ministers and prime ministers to seek their support for Singapore's bids. The then Kiribati President, Anote Tong, told me that he had read Lee Kuan Yew's book *From Third World to First*. Through the Tongan officials, I met my long-lost friend who was then the Lord Chamberlain after retiring from the Foreign Service. This trip enabled me to see the vulnerability of the lives and livelihoods of the South Pacific islanders. The soil in the islands cannot support much vegetation. The land is low-lying. There is no protection from the weather and climate change.

Then Minister Mentor Lee Kuan Yew, made a working visit to New Zealand in 2007. He told me the visit would be his last to New Zealand and he wished to visit several places that he had seen in his first visit. During his eight-day visit, Minister Mentor advised me to visit the French territories in the Pacific. I had already signed up earlier to visit New Caledonia, where the French government was trying to promote tourism. Participants paid for all expenses for the trip. I also had interest in the Pacific Island states in general because I met some of their diplomats in the Australian Foreign Service Course that I attended in 1980.

I visited New Caledonia, Tahiti, Fiji, Tonga, Samoa, Cook Islands and Kiribati. The French administered New Caledonia and Tahiti well. The ferries in Tahiti were the best. They were new, big and beautiful. Tahiti gets income from the rich and famous tourists, as well as oyster and pearl farms. Besides income from tourism, New Caledonia has a big nickel mine and the nickel is sent to France. In Tahiti, I met and talked to a Singaporean who is married to a local of Chinese descent working in the French administration

In our work, there are many challenging moments, even with consular problems. Air crashes and earthquakes happen at inconvenient times. In 2006, the duty officer in Singapore was apologetic when he called me at 4 o'clock in the morning to inform me that the BBC had reported an earthquake of magnitude 8 on the Richter scale in Tonga. I told him not to worry and that I would inform the Singaporeans living on the coast in New Zealand and in Fiji to be wary of the impending tsunami.

We deal with foreigners and Singaporeans. We must always have empathy, tact and courtesy when dealing with others. When I was Ambassador in Laos, the Australian Third Secretary called to inform me of an air crash in a northern province in which a Singaporean was killed. It is important to be helpful to the people we meet.

Promoting Singapore's Political, Economic, Security and Strategic Interests in its Relations with Thailand and Australia

by Tan Seng Chye

Communist Victories in South Vietnam, Cambodia and Laos in 1975 Posed Serious Challenges to Security of the Association of Southeast Asian Nations

I was assigned to the Singapore Embassy in late February 1975 and in a few months of my arrival in Bangkok, the three Indochinese states had fallen to the communists — Cambodia (17 March 1975), Vietnam (30 April 1975) and Laos later in the year. The Americans who supported the regimes in Phnom Penh, Saigon and Vientiane lost their wars to the communists in these states. These significant developments with the communist victories in Indochina posed a serious security threat and challenge to non-communist Association of Southeast Asian Nations (ASEAN), and they changed the geopolitical and geostrategic environment in Southeast Asia.

My assignment to Thailand from February 1975 till February 1982 as First Secretary and later Counsellor took place at a significant period in our relations with Thailand during the Cold War and the Vietnam War, and in working with the ASEAN countries to deal with the security threats from the Indochinese countries. It was a period of great uncertainty. Thailand, being the frontline state in ASEAN, faced a hostile Indochina with Vietnam declaring that it was the leader of a greater Indochina, and threatening to bring "genuine independence" to Southeast Asian countries. ASEAN was also facing serious communist insurgencies inside their respective countries which were supported by China. ASEAN, therefore, had to strongly support Thailand.

Thailand, a Southeast Asia Treaty Organisation (SEATO) member, provided a major air base Utapao and a naval base Sathahip in its Eastern province and a string of air bases in its Northeast provinces for the United States (US) to prosecute its war in Indochina. Thai troops also participated in the Vietnam War. In view of its involvement, Thailand was seriously concerned about the Vietnamese threat to its security. After the communist victories in Indochina, Thais demonstrated in front of the US Embassy calling on the American troops and military presence in Thai bases to leave Thailand, which the US forces did soon after.

Indochinese Refugees and Vietnamese Boat People

With the communist victories in Cambodia, Vietnam and Laos, Thailand faced a great inflow of refugees from the three countries through its borders and the flow of boat people through Thai waters to Southeast Asia. Following the Vietnamese invasion and occupation of Cambodia, the Chinese fought a war with the Vietnamese at Lang Son in Northeast Vietnam in early 1979. About a million Hoa people fled South Vietnam as boat people and this outflow heightened towards the end of 1978 and 1979, with about 250,000 going to China and the rest to Southeast Asia. The intended destinations were the US, Western countries and Australia, but their passage through the ASEAN countries posed serious problems as some had to be given temporary shelter in refugee camps while awaiting processing by the United Nations (UN) High Commissioner for Refugees and other UN agencies for resettlement to Western countries. This large outflow of Vietnamese boat people continued into the early 1990s. The Thai Navy and Coast Guard had to help the boat people if their rickety boats sank or stalled or were preyed upon by pirates. The boat people created enormous problems for the ASEAN countries.

Many of the refugees who chose to flee by land ended up in refugee camps in Thailand. About three million refugees flooded into East and Northeast Thailand, creating a humanitarian crisis for the Thai government and UN humanitarian aid agencies. Even in mid-1989, Thailand still hosted 419,000 refugees and displaced persons in its refugee camps.

ASEAN's Support for Thailand as a Frontline State

In the face of the growing threat, ASEAN countries had to maintain their unity to oppose Vietnam. The ASEAN Foreign Ministers held an urgent meeting in Bangkok from 11 to 12 January 1979 and issued an important statement to emphasise ASEAN's determination. Singapore played an active role together with other ASEAN countries in submitting a resolution in the UN General Assembly and other international fora calling for the withdrawal of Vietnamese forces from Cambodia and an end to its occupation of Cambodia.

In early 1981, Singapore initiated a meeting in Bangkok with the three Cambodian factions led by the late Prince Norodom Sihanouk of the National United Front for an Independent, Neutral, Peaceful and Cooperative Cambodia (FUNCINPEC);[1] the late Son Sann of the Khmer People's National Liberation Front (KPLNF) and the Khmer Rouge led by Khieu Samphan to establish the Coalition Government of Democratic Kampuchea (CGDK) headed by Prince Sihanouk as a united front to oppose Vietnam in the UN and international fora. The UN seat held by the Khmer Rouge Democratic Kampuchea was becoming untenable. The Singapore Embassy organised a meeting with the individual Cambodian factions in the Ambassador's residence that was not made known to the media. The three factions agreed to the proposed CGDK. The Singapore side was led by the late Deputy Prime Minister (DPM) S. Rajaratnam, along with the late Mr. S. R. Nathan and the late Ambassador Chi Owyang. I also attended the meeting. When it ended, at the request of Ambassador Chi, I arranged for then Thai Foreign Minister (FM) Siddhi Savetsila to be briefed by DPM Rajaratnam on the outcome of the meeting. The briefing was conducted at the Erawan Hotel, so as not to attract media attention. FM Siddhi was pleased to hear about the favourable

---

[1] FUNCINPEC is a French acronym for Front uni national pour un Cambodge indépendant, neutre, pacifique, et coopératif.

response of the Cambodian factions to the proposed CGDK, as it would serve as a more acceptable name of the Cambodian government at the UN and other international fora. This was a significant initiative by Singapore. Another meeting of the three factions was held in Singapore in early September 1981 to finalise the arrangement before the CGDK was officially launched by the Malaysian government in Kuala Lumpur with the presence of representatives of ASEAN countries on 22 June 1982. At their Annual Meeting on 25 June 1983, the ASEAN Foreign Ministers reiterated their conviction that the formation of the CGDK constituted a significant step towards a comprehensive political settlement of the Kampuchea problem.

Through ASEAN's strong lobbying efforts, international support for the ASEAN resolution grew with successive years in the UN and international fora and this contributed to Vietnam's isolation and eventual withdrawal of its forces following negotiations and conclusion of a UN-sponsored Paris Peace agreement in 1991. The CGDK was then renamed the National Government of Cambodia. ASEAN's role in helping to secure Vietnam's withdrawal enhanced ASEAN's image as an important regional organisation.

At the ASEAN and bilateral levels, Singapore had actively supported the Thai government in meeting the challenges that faced Thailand since the end of the Indochina War. Over these years, bilateral relations and cooperation had been strengthened as a result.

Promoting Trade and Economic Relations with Thailand

The situation in Thailand had stabilised after General Prem Tinsulanonda succeeded General Kriangsak Chomanan in March 1980. General Prem was credited with having ended the communist insurgencies and initiated the development of the economy in the mid-1980s.

Before I assumed my Ambassadorial post in March 1988, I consulted then Foreign Minister S. Dhanabalan and he agreed that I should promote economic and trade relations, as Thailand was developing its economy. The Thai Commerce Ministry, the Board of Trade and related economic agencies were all keen to strengthen bilateral trade and economic relations. Exchanges of trade and economic delegations were arranged. Singapore businesses were interested and with the support of the Thai economic ministries and business community, as well as support from representatives of Singapore companies in Bangkok, our Embassy arranged business matchmaking meetings with their Thai counterparts. In the relatively short time of two years, bilateral trade with and Singapore investments to Thailand rose to third and fourth positions in the trade and investments charts. The Singaporean business community also grew substantially. Singapore imported rice and other agricultural produce from Thailand.

Thailand also became an attractive destination for Singaporean tourists and with the Singapore Tourism Board promotions, bilateral tourism flourished.

Military Training in Thailand

The Singapore Armed Forces (SAF) has been doing a range of military training in Kanchana Buri since 1973 and this continues till today. Due to a lack of space in Singapore, the training facilities in Sai Yoke Camp are important to the SAF. The good relations between the two governments and the militaries have enabled the use of the training facilities in Thailand to continue for so many years.

Illegal Workers in Singapore

In March 1989, 10,000 illegal Thai workers were to be repatriated to Thailand. The Thai government expressed unhappiness about this repatriation and sent its Foreign Minister and the Deputy Interior Minister to negotiate. In view of the friendly bilateral relationship, Singapore eventually agreed to an amnesty repatriation whereby the Thai workers were allowed to return to Singapore if they complied with Singapore's immigration and work permit procedures. Normally illegal workers who were repatriated could not return to work in Singapore. The Thai government viewed the amnesty repatriation as a friendly gesture and the issue was amicably resolved.

Ambassador Chi's Role in Strengthening Bilateral Relations

During his 17-year tenure in Thailand (1971–1988), Ambassador Chi Owyang was able to strengthen ties with the Thai Royal Palace, the government leaders and officials and various sectors of Thai society. Mr. Nathan in his speech to the MFA Diplomatic Academy on 10 March 2008 praised Ambassador Owyang's contribution to the strengthening of relations with Thailand during his tenure. Ambassador Owyang's closeness to the Thai Royal Palace was legendary, and his friendship with succeeding generations of Thai leaders and the respect that Thai officials accorded him gave him access that other diplomats could only dream of.

Ambassador Owyang's National Day receptions held at the Dusit Thani Hotel Ball Room were always well attended by present and past Thai leaders and officials, military leaders and representatives from all sectors of Thai society and the business community. The Singapore National Day receptions were considered major social events in Bangkok.

When I succeeded Ambassador Owyang in March 1988, he remained as a Consultant with ambassadorial rank to the Embassy. As I was Ambassador Owyang's deputy in the Embassy from 1975 to early 1982, I had met almost all his contacts. As a result, when I hosted the National Day reception, the attendance was at the same level, reflecting the continuing close ties. During my tenure, I maintained warm and friendly relations with Thailand and made further progress in our bilateral trade and economic relations.

Promoting Political, Economic and Defence Relations with Australia

I was assigned as High Commissioner to Australia in October 1990. My priority was to promote political, economic and defence relations with Australia. With more than 5,000 Singapore students studying in all Australian states, cooperation in the education sector was progressing well. Bilateral tourism was growing. There were many Singaporeans in Australia, most of them doing business and some who had emigrated to Australia in the 1950s and 1960s. They maintained contact with the High

Commission and together with the students had established Singapore clubs or associations in most major Australian states. They used to invite the High Commissioner to attend their National Day celebrations.

Singapore has close relations with Australia as both are Commonwealth members and Australian soldiers had fought in Singapore during the Second World War. When Britain announced the withdrawal of its forces East of Suez, Australia, New Zealand, Malaysia, Singapore and the United Kingdom established the Five Power Defence Arrangements (FPDA) in 1971. FPDA members will consult in the event of a threat to any country and consider a joint response. The FPDA was established to ensure peace and stability in the Southeast Asia region.

During the Keating government, Singapore made significant progress in defence cooperation with the establishment of the RSAF Flying Training Institute at Pearce Base in Western Australia, and the RSAF fighter jets base in Darwin, Northern Territory in late 1993. During the typhoon season in December and January, our fighter jets would train at the Royal Australian Air Force (RAAF) Base in Richmond in New South Wales. Aside from army training exercises in Townsville, Queensland, the Keating government later offered armoured training at Shoalwater Bay area in Queensland. Due to a lack of land and airspace in Singapore, these training bases are important to the RSAF. These are significant developments in defence cooperation that strengthened the close bilateral relationship.

Singapore was also buying more agricultural products, especially fruits and vegetables and seafood from Australia. As the Australian dollar depreciated to being on par with the Singapore dollar in the early 1990s, bilateral trade and investments in Australia increased notably, especially in the hotel and office building sectors.

I completed my diplomatic assignment in December 1993 feeling that Singapore and Australia were enjoying friendly relations and multi-faceted cooperation and that significant progress has been made in defence cooperation in the training sector.

Observing Strategic and Security Issues — Diplomat on the Frontline

by Mushahid Ali

I was serving my national service as a Second Lieutenant in the Ministry of Defence in July/August 1969 when I was summoned by the Director, Security and Intelligence Division Mr. Tay Seow Hua, for an interview. There, I was told that I had been identified by the Ministry of Foreign Affairs (MFA), in particular by the late Parliamentary Secretary Mr. Rahim Ishak, as being suitable for the Foreign Service. I agreed to join MFA and was told to report for duty in January 1970. I had previously been a broadcast journalist covering Malaysian politics and had accompanied Malaysian Ministers on their tours, including the late Prime Minister (PM) Tunku Abdul Rahman and the late Deputy PM Tun Abdul Razak. Upon commencement of my service in MFA, I was naturally assigned to cover Malaysia.

Five Power Defence Arrangement — Lima Bersatu

Within a month of my appointment, I was posted to the Singapore High Commission in Kuala Lumpur (KL). An early milestone of my posting was when Singapore and Malaysia became members of the Five Power Defence Arrangement (FPDA) with the United Kingdom (UK), Australia and New Zealand in 1971. The FPDA was the successor to the Anglo-Malaya Defence Agreement (AMDA) in 1970 and included Malaysia and Singapore upon the latter's separation from Malaysia in 1965.

The FPDA was concluded by the late British Defence Secretary Peter Carrington on his visit to KL in 1971. The late Malaysian Foreign Secretary Ghazali Shafie briefed me on the Agreement, which committed the signatories to consult in case of an attack on any member. Ghazali called me up at the Southeast Asia Peninsular Games at the Merdeka Stadium (which I was attending in place of High Commissioner Maurice Baker). That brief meeting established my credentials as "second man" of the Singapore High Commission in KL soon after I had taken up the post.

I was invited to join the diplomatic delegation to travel by helicopter to the jungle location of the FPDA exercise (Lima Bersatu) in Trengganu as Singapore did not have a Defence Attache then. It was my first ride on a helicopter. I continued to engage diplomats from the FPDA countries as well as other Commonwealth countries, when we met socially as members of the Commonwealth Diplomatic Cricket Team which was headed by our First Secretary (Security Liaison); we met teams from the police, army and royalty from Negri Sembilan.

Second Malayan Communist Party Insurgency

During my posting in KL, we observed Malaysia's fight against the Malayan Communist Party (MCP) and its remnants operating in the northern half of the peninsula, along the central mountain range at the southern Thai border. Though the Malayan Emergency was declared over in 1960, occasional forays by MCP groups reflected the continuation of the insurgency in Perak and Pahang in which the Malaysian Field Force was engaged. Some elements of the MCP ventured into Selangor from 1968 and showed their presence by carrying out assassinations of senior police officers, chief among them being the late Inspector General Salleh in KL. Police tried to counter them with sweeps and roadblocks along the highways between KL, Negeri Sembilan and Pahang.

I went with a senior member of the Prime Minister's Office in 1972 on a visit to the outskirts of Raub, Pahang where elements of the MCP had been sighted. But the villagers told us that those night-time visitors had left after leaving their mark. There were no police checkpoints along the main roads between Kuantan and KL. The insurgency was finally ended by a peace treaty between the Malaysian government and MCP in 1989. The MCP remnants settled in southern Thailand.

Their leader, the late Chin Peng, was not permitted to return to Malaysia. However, he was able to visit Singapore in October 2004 and gave his view of the Emergency at a lecture which I attended. During the signing of his autobiography *My Side of History*, I asked him if he recalled one Wee Mon Cheng, the late Singapore Ambassador to Japan. Chin Peng responded warmly, saying that Wee had been his mentor. He asked to meet him and was disappointed when I told him that Wee had passed away. Wee had been a teacher in a school in Perak where Chin Peng was a young member of the MCP's Anti-British League. During Chin Peng's visit to Singapore, I gathered that he had been able to meet some Singapore leaders including the late Mr. Lee Kuan Yew. He died a few years later in southern Thailand.

Security Observer: Palestine Liberation Organization and Japanese Red Army

Following the Arab–Israeli war in October 1973, I observed a massive demonstration on the High Street close to our High Commission in KL against the United States (US). The demonstrators, led by Muslim youth leaders Anwar Ibrahim and Hishamuddin Rais, threw stones at the Lincoln Centre library before proceeding to the US Embassy, where they lowered the American flag. The march halted after Ghazali invited the leaders to meet him for talks at the National Mosque nearby.

Two other security incidents followed in January 1974: an attack on the Embassy of Japan in KL, where the Palestine Liberation Organization (PLO) and Japanese Red Army demanded a flight out to Kuwait, and the other on the Shell refinery at Pulau Bukom in Singapore which was accompanied by the seizure of the Laju ferry by Palestinian and Japanese hijackers. The Laju hijack, which lasted nine days, ended when the hijackers agreed to being escorted out on a Japan Airlines flight to Kuwait in return for the release of the Laju ferry crew. The Singapore escorting team was led by the late S. R. Nathan, who then headed the Home Affairs Ministry.

I had been alerted by the PLO representative in KL about the attack some months earlier. He warned me that although the PLO had no quarrel with Singapore, they were planning an attack in Singapore to advance their cause. No date was specified, but I informed Singapore MFA through a secret telex about the warning. The attack took place in January 1974. It was a lesson that Singapore was vulnerable to attacks by external forces, even though Singapore was not involved in any conflict or disputes abroad.

A similar episode occurred when the late Israeli President Chaim Herzog visited Singapore in 1986. I was Counsellor at the Singapore Embassy in Jakarta at the time. Muslim groups in Indonesia and Malaysia expressed their displeasure with demonstrations against the visit in both countries. However, a threatened protest against the Singapore Embassy in Jakarta did not materialise, thanks to the intervention of the late Indonesian security chief, Benny Moerdani, after I had a word with him.

Interestingly, in contrast, there were no demonstrations when the late Israeli Prime Minister Yitzhak Rabin made an unannounced visit to Singapore in 1992. As Chief of Protocol, I looked after PM Rabin during his low-key programme. We arranged for him to stay at the Shangri-la Hotel and provided him with a discreet escort when he went for a stroll along Orchard Road, it being a Sabbath and PM Rabin was not able to ride a vehicle. The late Senior Minister Lee Kuan Yew called on him in the hotel, while he met then PM Goh Chok Tong at the Istana Villa on the evening before his departure.[1] We were preparing to give a similar welcome to the late PLO Leader Yasser Arafat on his way to Indonesia, but the visit was called off.

Malaysia–China Relations

Malaysia responded to China's overtures to establish relations from the early 1970s after it switched diplomatic recognition from Taipei to Beijing. The late Malaysian PM Tun Abdul Razak visited China in 1974 to establish diplomatic relations and met the late Chairman Mao Zedong and the late Premier Zhou Enlai. That boosted his image among the ethnic

---

[1] Rabin graciously posed for a photograph with me when I saw him off at Changi Airport.

Chinese population of Malaysia. I followed this development closely while serving at the High Commission in KL and was able to forecast the timing quite accurately, even though I had left KL a few months before PM Razak's visit to Beijing.

Gulf Conflict — Iraqi Invasion of Kuwait

I was on the frontline of the Gulf conflict in 1990/91, which began with the Iraqi invasion of Kuwait on 1 August 1990, when I was Head of Mission in Riyadh. We observed the flight of Kuwaiti notables into Saudi Arabia and prepared for the threat of Iraqi forces crossing the border into Saudi territory. As the Kuwaiti refugees were given accommodation in hotels in Riyadh, foreign nationals prepared to evacuate to their home countries, including Singapore. Our Mission coordinated the evacuation of Singaporeans in Saudi Arabia and the other Gulf states.

Anticipating the Iraqi invasion of Saudi Arabia, the 30-strong allied coalition opposing the Iraqi forces took steps to evacuate their nationals as well. Singapore was part of the coalition, having sent over a military medical team. I represented Singapore at the signing of an agreement with the Commander of the Saudi forces and liaised with the coalition command on logistics. We arranged for the Republic of Singapore Air Force to fly out a score of Singaporeans and Bruneians on the return flight of the aircraft that brought in the Singapore Armed Forces medical contingent in mid-January 1991.

The coalition launched a massive air campaign against Iraqi forces on 17 January 1991. The air attacks went on until late February, during which Iraqi forces launched Scud missile attacks on Saudi Arabia including Riyadh, which we observed from our homes. Two of the missiles found Saudi targets — one an immigration building in Riyadh and the other a US troop concentration in Dahran, resulting in several casualties. However, the US and allied forces did not have to engage the shell-shocked Iraqi forces, who duly surrendered on 28 February 1991. I was among the diplomats invited to the victory celebration attended by the Commander of the coalition forces, the late General Norman Schwarzkopf, and another victory parade mounted by the Saudi Armed Forces in Dammam a week later.

Iran–Iraq War

One of the most bitter conflicts in the Middle East was the war between Iran and Iraq that lasted for eight years from 1980 to 1988. It started when Iraq seized control of the Shat-el-Arab waterway along the Iran border and launched an artillery attack across the canal in 1980. Iran responded with its own artillery barrage and a full-scale counterattack on Iraq, which Iraqi forces returned in kind. Both sides suffered heavy casualties, resulting in one million troops killed on each side, until they called a halt to the fighting when an Iranian civilian airliner was shot down over the Persian Gulf in 1988.

Before that the Iraqis acquired long-range East Wind missiles that Saudi Arabia had purchased for them from China. I was Head of Mission in Riyadh when the missiles were delivered and observed the support given to Iraq by the Arab states. Iran was isolated and had no diplomatic presence in Riyadh. I saw some Iranian representatives at the Haj pilgrimage in Mecca, where some of their pilgrims mounted demonstrations against Israel at the Holy Mosque. The Iran–Iraq conflict showed the limits of diplomacy, when two antagonists were at war and no outside powers were involved until the end.

Vietnam's Invasion of Cambodia

The Association of Southeast Asian Nations (ASEAN) faced a major strategic challenge when Vietnam invaded Cambodia in December 1978. Although neither was a member of ASEAN, Singapore and Thailand raised the alarm that the invasion and occupation of Cambodia threatened the security of all states in Southeast Asia, in particular neighbouring Thailand. It was not just a border conflict between Vietnam and Cambodia, which they had been engaged in the previous year, but was a violation of the universal principle that no country should use force or violence against another, especially a large country against a smaller neighbour. Vietnam had claimed that it had acted in self-defence against Cambodia's attacks on Vietnam's border region. Vietnam's superior armed forces had overwhelmed Cambodia's much-weakened forces following the Khmer Rouge's brutal rule involving two years and more of genocide.

Singapore led ASEAN in opposing Vietnam's aggression and marshalled the international community to condemn the invasion and occupation of Cambodia. While the diplomatic offensive was centred at the United Nations (UN) General Assembly with its annual vote against Vietnam, Singapore and several ASEAN allies helped to mobilise Cambodia's resistance. Singapore also took the lead in organising an international conference on Cambodia at the UN. Our diplomats to the UN, and in the US, UK and European Union, actively lobbied for their host countries' support.

I was involved in liaising with the UK and Indonesia's Foreign Ministries and communicating with Vietnamese diplomats in Jakarta, including arranging for Vietnam's Foreign Minister, the late Nguyen Co Thach, to meet Singapore's Foreign Minister during a stopover from Jakarta. I worked with the Singapore delegation that met the US Secretary of State George Schultz in Jakarta during the ASEAN Foreign Ministers meeting in 1984 to coordinate their collaboration in forming the Friends of Cambodia that intensified the opposition against Vietnam. The united front achieved a successful conclusion in late 1989 when Vietnamese forces withdrew from Cambodia following the withdrawal of the Soviet Union from its occupation of Afghanistan.

China–Vietnam War

The Vietnam–Cambodia conflict was followed by the war between China and Vietnam that broke out on 17 February 1979 when China bombarded Vietnam's border region at Langson with artillery and tanks. The Vietnamese forces returned fire from entrenched defences and the battles continued through the next two weeks. As Chinese armoured divisions ventured further into Vietnam's northern region, they were repulsed by Vietnam's artillery. The conflict ended when Chinese forces withdrew after declaring they had achieved their objective to teach the Vietnamese a lesson, while Vietnam likewise claimed it had inflicted heavy punishment on Chinese forces across the border.

The China–Vietnam border war was preceded by diplomatic forays by Vietnam and China to Southeast Asian states in November 1978. Vietnam's PM, the late Pham Van Dong, visited Malaysia, Indonesia and

Singapore, while the late Chinese Vice-Premier Deng Xiaoping visited Thailand, Malaysia and Singapore. I was involved in the visits of Vice-Premier Deng and PM Dong and subsequently in monitoring the war between China and Vietnam.

Cambodian Coalition Conflict

When I was serving as Ambassador to Cambodia, a bitter short-lived conflict between Cambodia's coalition partners the National United Front for an Independent, Neutral, Peaceful and Cooperative Cambodia (FUNCINPEC) and the Cambodian People's Party (CPP) broke out in June 1996 with an exchange of artillery fire between the headquarters of the two parties. Some FUNCINPEC leaders sought refuge in my residence which was located close to their homes as other FUNCINPEC leaders left for Paris before the fighting started. CCP Hun Sen's forces surrounded the FUNCINPEC headquarters until they called a halt to the fighting. Hun Sen had gone to a resort in South Vietnam. He flew back to Phnom Penh the next day and took control of Cambodia.

ASEAN AND SINGAPORE

Working at the ASEAN Level

by Ong Keng Yong

I joined the Singapore Foreign Service in 1979 after graduation from the Law School in the National University of Singapore. Following my diplomatic postings in Saudi Arabia, Malaysia, the United States, India and Nepal, I became the 11th Secretary-General of the Association of Southeast Asian Nations (ASEAN) from 1 January 2003 to 31 December 2007. I was based at the ASEAN Secretariat (ASEC) in Jakarta, Indonesia.

ASEAN protocol is that the Secretary-General will take over (and hand over) responsibilities at a specific ceremony at ASEC presided over by the Foreign Minister of Indonesia. This originated from the recognition of Indonesia by the other founding member states of ASEAN (Malaysia, the Philippines, Singapore and Thailand) as the largest country and economy in Southeast Asia, and the decision of then President of Indonesia, Suharto, to host the ASEAN Secretariat in his capital city. Officially, I assumed the post of Secretary-General of ASEAN on 6 January 2003 and relinquished it on 7 January 2008 in the presence of then Indonesian Foreign Minister Hassan Wirajuda (who was in office from 2001 to 2009).

Previously, Mr. Chan Kai Yau was the only other Singaporean who served as Secretary-General of ASEAN (from July 1982 to July 1984). At that time, the job was more limited, and the stint was for two to three years each round. ASEAN leaders broadened the mandate of the Secretary-General in 1992 and accorded the office-holder full ministerial status with a fixed term of five years each time from January 1993 when the late Malaysian diplomat Ajit Singh took over the helm. He was succeeded by the late Rodolfo Severino of the Philippines in January 1998, and I took over from the latter in January 2003. The rotation was based on the alphabetical order of the English names of the ASEAN Member States (AMS).

Before I went to Jakarta, I had the opportunity to ask the late Mr. Lee Kuan Yew what I should focus on in my ASEAN job. He replied, "Do what we can for ASEAN. It is useful for us. It is the only one we have. Good luck." A few short sentences! Clearly to me, they meant ASEAN is the only regional organisation in Southeast Asia and it is important for Singapore's interests.

Prior to the ASEAN assignment, I was seconded out of the Ministry of Foreign Affairs (MFA) to work as Press Secretary to then Prime Minister (PM) Goh Chok Tong while serving concurrently as the Chief Executive Director (CED) of the People's Association whose Chairman is the PM. I asked PM Goh what was expected of me in the ASEAN job. His reply: "It is important to get Singaporeans more aware of the value of ASEAN. Our officials tend to be clinical and impatient with ASEAN — a lot of eating, golfing, singing, and travelling. Other Southeast Asians are watching Singaporeans — to see if we are sincere and willing to do more for ASEAN."

PM Goh pointed out that Singapore would always be different from the rest of Southeast Asia, and I could help to explain that to the people in other AMS so that there could be more understanding of Singapore and its policy. On substantive matters, he said that MFA should brief me from time to time, but MFA must not behave like "bossing the Secretary-General of ASEAN around" as that would make my job even more difficult. It would be best that I speak up objectively on Singapore's stand on specific issues in ASEAN. The bottom line was to treat all the AMS, including Singapore, equally and fairly.

There was high expectation within the rank and file of ASEC with my appointment as Secretary-General of ASEAN. First, Singapore was always regarded as a "no-nonsense" member state which would speak out or act whenever there was an issue Singapore could not accept or agree with. Singapore's reputation as an efficient government would mean a Secretary-General who would make the Secretariat more professional and dynamic.

Second, many believed that the Secretary-General from Singapore would have a plan to do something new and special to distinguish his term from that of his predecessors. This feeling was fanned by talks in ASEAN circles that the Singapore government would provide more resources for the Initiative for ASEAN Integration (IAI) projects. The fact that I was Press Secretary to PM Goh Chok Tong reinforced this view. He was widely regarded in ASEAN, especially in Cambodia, Laos, Myanmar and Viet Nam (CLMV), as the originator of IAI which focused on narrowing the development gap among the AMS.

Third, my youthfulness (49 years old then) and the youngest man to take the top job in ASEAN was regarded as a sea change. The sense of the ASEC staff was that as a younger serving diplomat, I would be proactive and be present at many ASEAN meetings to provide the necessary backing for secretariat support rendered by ASEC. The personnel in the ASEC Public Relations Office also spread the story that I would be comfortable dealing with the mass media and speaking in public.

Hanging Together

Some experts claimed that the top-down nature of ASEAN decision-making, based on consensus and consultation, created an insurmountable obstacle going forward. Yet, ASEAN supporters argued that ASEAN is not unique in this respect. The problem is the belief among individual AMS that they need not change their respective national systems and operational ways to be in ASEAN. Some of them pointed to the ASEAN agreement on specific issues when the AMS could give and take on the lowest common denominator. However, the question should be "Is this enough?" Imagine the possibilities open to ASEAN acting in unison and tackling the challenges confronting them.

I often stated the need for 10 countries "hanging together or be hung separately". There is more harm to the national interests of individual AMS if ASEAN is in disarray. There is a sense that the AMS make decisions on short-term political expediency instead of the long-term well-being of ASEAN. AMS leaders and senior officials are seen speaking up on issues only when the interests of their respective countries are directly involved. Not many officials will intervene to promote consensus and bring about a generally useful outcome for a particular ASEAN cause or project, especially those in the non-economic sectors.

This does not mean Singapore and other AMS cannot work together in specific areas where there is mutuality of interests. The best example is the cooperation in concluding free trade agreements (FTAs) with ASEAN's key trading partners. Singapore collaborated with Malaysia to advance ASEAN economic integration as the two countries leverage each other's comparative strength to push the other Member States to join the FTA bandwagon. To be sure, much of this collaboration also originated from the good personal relationship between senior civil servants of Singapore and Malaysia.

Looking ahead, Singapore must find ways to work the ASEAN processes more purposefully to help Singapore protect and advance its own interests. In fact, Singapore has helped fellow Member States: in the IAI projects and the ASEAN Master Plan on Connectivity. Unfortunately, the other AMS see Singapore's principled stand (e.g., equal contributions to the ASEC budget) as selfish moves. Singapore officials must avoid coming across as ignorant of the promise of ASEAN. Singapore is considered a successful country with a remarkable capacity in problem-solving by the AMS and ASEAN Dialogue Partners. Singapore must maintain this positive image.

As an ASEAN expert working at the Asian Development Bank put it: "What we get from ASEAN is not black and white." Frequently, AMS work tediously behind the public eyes and media glare to reach a workable arrangement for political, economic and socio-cultural cooperation. Some people think this is a horrible way to operate a regional body. Yet, most thinking persons appreciate the logic of such a model as no country will join an organisation and be bound by the decision of the body at the expense of sovereign independence.

A favourite statement in most ASEAN negotiations is "seeking the low-hanging fruit". It is the starting point to do more together as a collective. The challenge is to present this low-hanging fruit in a manner that all member states can take home to satisfy domestic constituencies and protect the respective national interests. But in the first place, what is the low-hanging fruit? This means many negotiating sessions and a good understanding of policy nuances and operational sensitivities in each member state.

Usually, on sensitive or strategic issues, ASEAN officials danced around the fire many times before all the individual bits can be put into a viable option for all to buy in. In this process, the chairman or host is most important — to converge different positions, refine the possibilities and recommend appropriate action to go forward. The Secretary-General of ASEAN plays a crucial role in supporting the chairman/host, pushing the envelope where needed and sealing the conclusion expeditiously for the next stage.

Not Knowing Enough

During the five years I was Secretary-General of ASEAN, I found that Singapore was perceived by fellow AMS as thinking too fast and too far ahead, thereby coming across often as being impatient and pushy. Some quarters claimed that Singaporeans had little appreciation of how other AMS work, and there had been occasional pushback over Singapore's impatience and insensitivity. When Singapore officials go to the ASEAN Summit, on a personal leader-to-leader approach, to expedite decision-making on specific issues, the implementation of what would be agreed at the top could be stretched out unduly by bureaucrats on the ground in different AMS.

It is not always natural for Singapore officials to include ASEAN concerns and initiatives in their respective policy deliberations at home. While more attention is being paid today to the ASEAN agenda, especially the building of the ASEAN Community, there remain unsatisfactory knowledge of ASEAN, its value and its work processes vis-à-vis Singapore's own development plans and long-term goals. In essence, the potentiality of ASEAN is inadequately appreciated by various decision-makers in Singapore's public, private and people sectors.

As Secretary-General of ASEAN (and even today, 14 years after I left that post), I spent a significant amount of time to explain ASEAN and its programmes/vision to Singaporeans, particularly those in the policy domain. Even so, ASEAN continues to be neglected by many Singaporeans. Our neighbours are frustrated by the better knowledge of other countries farther away among Singaporeans than the unique Southeast Asian traits and traditions.

I had avoided pushing the "efficient and slick ways of the Singapore system" (as my ASEAN friends described it) when I was Secretary-General of ASEAN. I stressed that the Singaporean way of working was based on accepted international standards and practices. I introduced work procedures and performance measurements from the International Organization for Standardization (ISO) into ASEC. I strengthened the "technical officers" corps in the ASEAN Secretariat, offering them scholarships to do advance studies abroad and returning with better professional qualifications for their respective roles in ASEC. I expanded the "attachment scheme" for young officials covering ASEAN portfolios from the newer AMS, namely, Cambodia, Laos, Myanmar and Vietnam.

I retained experienced and productive staff members rather than following the old scheme of them placed on employment at ASEC for a fixed term (of say six or seven years) and letting them leave, taking their expertise and skills with them. Consequently, several seasoned staff members were able to continue their employment at ASEC. They brought solid contribution to the eventual setting up of the ASEAN Charter and the ASEAN Community.

Moving Forward

My references to certain aspects of my encounters as Secretary-General of ASEAN are meant to illustrate Singapore's possible contribution to strengthening ASEAN capacity and capability as a functioning regional body. Human resources are essential for the future growth of ASEAN. Singapore can help to maximise the potential of Southeast Asians in tackling the challenges facing them. In the process, Singapore's standing in the eyes of the ASEAN Community will be enhanced.

In closing, it must be acknowledged that many major decisions and initiatives of ASEAN depend on the force of personality involved. Individual leaders and advocates of specific causes matter for the success of anything which ASEAN is doing. During my time as Secretary-General of ASEAN, three women created significant impact on the ASEAN agenda: Megawati Sukarnoputri, Gloria Macapagal-Arroyo and Rafidah Aziz.

Without the relatively benign approach of Megawati towards ASEAN, we would not have the launching of the ASEAN Community so quickly. Without the dogged determination of Arroyo, we would not have the ASEAN Declaration on the Promotion and Protection of the Rights of Migrant Workers (which removed a huge bone of contention among several Member States). Without the cajoling ways of Rafidah, the ASEAN economic officials might not have delivered on the concrete outcome of the FTA negotiations as they eventually did.

▲ Singapore's historic relations with Britain matured with Singapore's fast-paced development. The tenor of the relationship has evolved to high-tech partnership cooperation in broad areas of mutual interest e.g., financial hub services, global security issues and more. Visits by Queen Elizabeth II and other dignitaries served to strengthen the strategic partnership.

Picture courtesy of V.K. Rajan, Serving Singapore: My Journey, p. 224.

▲ President Suharto's wise counsel and rule gave peace and stability to Indonesia and the region. Here, Indonesia's President paid an official visit to Singapore in 1987, having arrived via the causeway from Malaysia. He is shaking hands with Minister for Trade and Industry and Second Minister for Defence Lee Hsien Loong, accompanied by Singapore's Chief of Protocol, V.K. Rajan.

Picture courtesy of V.K. Rajan.

▲ Singapore delegation to the 1989 Paris Conference on Cambodia.
(Back Row) Ambassador to Paris David Marshall, MINDEF Research Analyst Tan York Chor (later Ambassador to Paris, 2011–2015) and MFA Director for Southeast Asia Bilahari Kausikan. (Front Row) Aun Koh (Intern to the French Paris Conference Secretariat), Professor Chan Heng Chee, Foreign Minister Wong Kan Seng, MFA Permanent Secretary Peter Chan, Counsellor of the Singapore Embassy in Washington, D.C. Ms. Lee Yoke Kwang, Counsellor of the Singapore Embassy in Paris Ms. Joyce Davamoni and Ambassador to the United States of America Tommy Koh.

Picture courtesy of Tan York Chor.

▲ Ambassador-at-Large Tommy Koh was appointed the UN Secretary-General's Special Envoy in 1993 to negotiate the withdrawal of Russian troops from the Baltic States. He is in Estonia, at the residence of President Lennart Meri, who hosted the delegation to lunch.

Picture courtesy of Tommy Koh.

▲ Ambassador to Jakarta Barry Desker and Mrs. Desker receiving Admiral Sudomo, Indonesian Minister for Political and Security Affairs, at the Singapore National Day Reception, 1988.

Picture courtesy of Barry Desker.

▲ High Commissioner Low Choon Ming (centre) with Singapore pensioners living in Malaysia at the National Day celebration in the Singapore High Commission in Kuala Lumpur in 1990. First on the left is Deputy Chief of Mission Ong Keng Yong and on the far right is First Secretary R. Raj Kumar.

Picture courtesy of R. Raj Kumar.

▲ Culture diplomacy at its best. *Singapour en France: Les Festivarts*, 1000 Singapores exhibition, at the Cite de l'Architecture, Paris in celebration of the 50th Anniversary of Singapore–France relations. Members of the Singapore Symphony Children's Choir (who performed Belioz's Concert Te Deum at the Philharmonie de Paris as an event of the Festivarts). Minister of State Sam Tan is in the middle of the middle row, with Ambassador Tan York Chor to MOS Tan's left. National Heritage Board Chief Executive Rosa Daniel is on Ambassador Tan's left.

Picture courtesy of Tan York Chor.

▲ Helicopter Tour of the giga-sized NEOM Project by Ambassadors and their spouses in Tabuk Province, northwestern Saudi Arabia. Ambassador Lawrence Anderson and his wife Maureen are 9th and 10th in line from the left, respectively. The name "NEOM" is based on two words — the first three letters 'NEO' form the Ancient Greek prefix νέο Neo — meaning "new". The fourth letter 'M' is from the abbreviation of Arabic: لبقتسم, romanised: Mustaqbal, the Arabic word for 'future.' NEOM covers an area 31 times the size of Singapore.

Picture courtesy of Lawrence Anderson.

▲ High Commissioner Bernard Baker with then Governor General of New Zealand, Sir Jerry Mateparae.

Picture courtesy of Bernard Baker.

▲ Camaraderie amongst retired MFA colleagues, reflecting on past 'war stories' perhaps?
From left: R. Raj Kumar, Anson Chua, Lee Chiong Giam, Ajit Singh, Lim Cheng Hoe, Jimmy Chua.

Picture courtesy of Anson Chua.

▲ In the aftermath of Cyclone Nargis, Ambassador Robert Chua receives the Singapore Medical Team at Yangon Airport in May 2008.

Picture courtesy of Robert Chua.

▲ Singapore's Non-Resident High Commissioner to the Republic of Rwanda, Mr Yatiman Yusof and wife, with President Paul Kagame of the Republic of Rwanda, after the Presentation of Credentials Ceremony.

Picture courtesy of Yatiman Yusof.

▲ Ambassador Ong Keng Yong (Singapore) was the 11th Secretary-General (SG) of ASEAN for five years (2003–2007). In the photo with him (from left): 9th SG of ASEAN (1993–1997) Tan Sri Ajit Singh (Malaysia), 13th SG of ASEAN (2013–2017) Ambassador Le Luong Minh (Vietnam) and 14th SG of ASEAN (2018–2022) Dato Lim Jock Hoi (Brunei Darussalam). Together, they formed the ASEAN Prize Judging Committee which annually selects an outstanding individual or institution from the ASEAN Member States in recognition of splendid work done for the well-being of the ASEAN Community. In the background are photo portraits of other Secretaries-General of ASEAN.

Picture courtesy of ASEAN Secretariat in Jakarta.

▲ The Singapore Delegation members to the High Level Task Force on the Drafting of the ASEAN Charter in 2007 included Ambassador-at-Large Tommy Koh (sixth from left) and Ambassador to Brussels Walter Woon (extreme right). ASEAN Secretary-General Ong Keng Yong is standing next to Ambassador Woon.

Picture courtesy of Ong Keng Yong.

▲ State Visit to Singapore by Japanese Emperor Akihito and Empress Michiko, June 2006. President Nathan and Mrs. Nathan receiving the Royal guests at the Istana.

Picture courtesy of the Ministry of Communications and Information.

▲ Welcome Ceremony for President and Mrs. Nathan by the Emperor & Empress of Japan at the Imperial Palace, May 2009. Ambassador Tan Chin Tiong is third from the left.

Picture courtesy of Tan Chin Tiong.

▲ Singapore's Minister-in-charge of Trade Relations S. Iswaran and Maharashtra Chief Minister Devendra Fadnavis signed a framework agreement to facilitate Singapore investments in Maharashtra in May 2018. Singapore Consul General Ajit Singh is on the extreme right.

Picture courtesy of Ajit Singh.

▲ Singapore Heads of Mission Meeting with Emeritus Senior Minister Goh Chok Tong at the Istana, 2015.

Picture courtesy of the Ministry of Communications and Information.

▲ Singapore Heads of Mission's discussion with Prime Minister Lee Hsien Loong at the Istana, 2015.

Picture courtesy of the Ministry of Communications and Information.

▲ Ambassador A. Selverajah meeting Turkish President Recep Tayyip Erdoğan in Ankara on 15 September 2015.

Picture courtesy of the Singapore Embassy in Ankara.

▲ Non-Resident Ambassador to the Vatican Barry Desker at his Presentation of Credentials Ceremony, December 2007. Picture shows Pope Benedict greeting Mrs. Desker, with Ambassador Desker in the centre.

Picture courtesy of © Vatican Media.

▲ Staying connected with and looking after the interests of Singaporeans abroad is a key consideration of all Singapore Embassies. Here, Tan Lian Choo, Singapore's first Head of Mission in Brasilia, is celebrating National Day with fellow Singaporeans in São Paulo, Brazil.

Picture courtesy of Sumaya Baqavi.

OUR GLOBAL REACH

Japan and Singapore: Growing Ties

by Tan Chin Tiong

I retired in June 2004 after seven years as Permanent Secretary in the Ministry of Foreign Affairs (MFA). On 2 November, I presented credentials to Emperor Akihito at the Imperial Palace as Singapore's ninth Ambassador to Japan.

Substantive Collaborations

Our relations with Japan were excellent. Over the years, Singapore's political leaders, in particular late Prime Minister (PM) Lee Kuan Yew and our Ambassadors and officials, had assiduously built up our cooperative ties with Japan. Recent examples of our substantive collaboration include the Japan–Singapore Free Trade Agreement (JSFTA), a first for Japan concluded in 2002, encouraging more Japanese investments into Singapore. The Japanese Maritime Self-Defence Force (JMSDF) was the second largest user of Changi Naval Base after the United States (US) Navy.

In October 2004, Japan's Ministry of Foreign Affairs (Gaimusho) finalised the Regional Cooperation Agreement on Combating Piracy and Armed Robbery (ReCAAP)[1] with 12 Asian countries in Tokyo. In November 2006, Japan decided to locate the Information Sharing Centre (ISC) in Singapore, thus enhancing our role as a regional maritime hub.

---

[1] ReCAAP is the first regional government-to-government agreement to promote and enhance cooperation against piracy and armed robbery in Asia. Founding members include Brunei, Cambodia, Laos, Myanmar, Philippines, Japan, China, Republic of Korea, India, Sri Lanka, Singapore and Thailand. In 2005, Indonesia and Malaysia pledged their countries' cooperation with the centre.

Singapore worked closely with Japan to enlarge the Association of Southeast Asian Nations (ASEAN) Plus Three (APT) grouping[2] to include India, Australia and New Zealand. The ASEAN Plus Six (East Asian Summit, EAS) was inaugurated in December 2005. In a further expansion in 2011, the US and Russia also joined the EAS.

Access to High Officials

A very important factor in our growing ties with Japan was trust among officials of both countries. Access to high officials of departments and ministries was important for the work of an ambassador. I also had a head start. Before my departure for Japan, George Yeo, then Minister for Trade and Industry, introduced me over dinner to Shoichi Nakagawa, his good friend who was then Japan's Trade Minister (METI). Nakagawa invited me to call on him when I arrived in Tokyo. This eased the way for calls on his Vice-Minister and Directors-General. Gaimusho officials gave me ready access as I had previously worked with them on various matters as MFA Permanent Secretary.

The Japan–Singapore Inter-Parliamentary Group of younger generation politicians from the ruling Liberal Democratic Party (LDP), the Democratic People's Party (DPP), Kōmeitō and others provided another channel for me to build relationships with these politicians to better understand Japan. This Group had been formed with the encouragement of PM Goh Chok Tong to foster interaction among younger politicians of both countries.

Among officials, I was fortunate to be introduced early to Yutaka Kawashima. He had been Administrative Vice Minister (Permanent Secretary) in Gaimusho before he joined the Imperial Household Grand Agency (Kunaichō) as Grand Master of Ceremonies (later as Grand Chamberlain to the Emperor). In this capacity, he coordinated the Emperor's overseas visit schedules as well as diplomatic meetings with Gaimusho. We became good friends because of our shared backgrounds as Permanent Secretaries.

---

[2] The APT, an informal summit among the leaders of ASEAN and China, Japan and the Republic of Korea, was first held in December 1997 on the sidelines of the 2nd ASEAN Informal Summit in Malaysia. It was only at its third meeting, held in Manila in 1999, that APT was institutionalised.

In early 2005, over dinner my wife and I hosted for him and his wife, he confided that the Emperor planned to be in Southeast Asia to attend the 60th anniversary celebrations of the late Thai King Bhumibol Adulyadej's reign the following year at which royals and dignitaries from other countries had been invited. Kawashima explained that the Emperor travelled overseas only once or twice a year, and it would be to several countries in the same region. Hence, the visit to Thailand would be coupled with another to Perak state in Malaysia where an earlier visit there had to be aborted because weather conditions made landing at the state airport unsafe. This was very important information because it gave us an opportunity to pitch for Singapore to be included. With the Ministry's approval, I followed up with a letter to him to convey our invitation.

A few months later, Kunai-chō announced that the Emperor and Empress would be making state visits to Thailand, Singapore and Malaysia in 2006.

State Visit by Emperor Akihito and Empress Michiko (8–10 June 2006)

The news that the Emperor and Empress would visit Singapore in June 2006 was the cause for celebration. After 39 years of diplomatic relations, this would be the first State Visit by the Emperor and Empress of Japan. Singaporeans and visitors alike welcomed the Imperial couple warmly. Media coverage was warm and friendly.

The State Visit included two events that the Emperor and Empress experienced during their visit to Singapore in 1970 as Crown Prince and Princess. Together with hosts PM Lee and Mrs. Lee, they had viewed the Southern Cross from the Istana rooftop. The second event involved planting two sago palms at the Japanese Gardens in the Jurong Lake area.

During the June 2006 State Visit, viewing was impossible because of heavy rain. The visit to the Japanese Gardens in Jurong Lake to view the palms brought back fond memories. Both palms had grown tall and luxuriant. The local Japanese community together with a delegation from Mihama City, Nagoya, which had been designated Singapore's sister city for the 2005 World Exposition (Aichi Banpaku) in Nagoya, were at the Gardens to greet the Imperial couple.

The State Visit was a milestone in our bilateral relations.

Showcasing Japanese Technology and Soft Power

Shinzō Abe became PM in July 2006. He formed an Asian Gateway Vision Committee, led by his special assistant, Takumi Nemoto (an up-and-coming Parliamentarian) to discuss with Asian ambassadors based in Tokyo how to build close relationships between Japan and Asia. We proposed a Japan Creative Centre[3] in Singapore to showcase Japan's technology. Such a centre would be a first for Japan as it had only cultural centres under the charge of the Japan Foundation. Gaimusho was lukewarm as technology did not come under its purview. We convinced Nemoto who took it directly to his PM to secure his approval. As a result, PM Lee Hsien Loong and PM Abe were able to announce this as a joint project when PM Lee made an official visit to Japan in March 2007.

People-to-People Links

In 2005, from 25 March to 25 September, the World Exposition (Banpaku) was held in Nagoya, Aichi Prefecture where Toyota Motors had its main manufacturing activities. A total of 121 countries participated. Countries hosting a pavilion at the Banpaku were paired to a local sister city. Mihama, our sister city of 10,000 people, was chosen because in 1862, the late Yamamoto Otokichi from Mihama was the first Japanese to settle in Singapore. Mihama's Mayor Yoichi Saito supported us with logistics, personnel and its local network. Together with the Chubu–Singapore and Hakodate–Singapore Friendship Associations led by Masashi Miyazaki and the late Masaru Yanagisawa, respectively, they deployed their communities' resources to support us. Our pavilion, Urban Nature, managed by the Singapore Tourism Board (STB) officials, featured a tropical rainfall setting that attracted a million visitors. It was one of the few pavilions selected for a visit by the Emperor and Empress of Japan.

The work of our friendship associations built up over the years by my predecessors was instrumental in extending our Embassy's outreach to

---

[3] In November 2009, the Japan Creative Centre (JCC) was established. It was housed in a conserved black and white bungalow at 4 Nassim Road in the Orchard Road area provided by Singapore.

local communities. Its members include Japanese who had worked in Singapore and Singaporeans married to Japanese or working in Singapore. In addition to Mihama, Chuba and Hokkaido, there were friendship associations in Osaka, Hiroshima, Nagasaki, Nagoya and Kyushu. This helped to encourage many Japanese visitors to visit our Pavilion.

State Visit to Japan by the late President S. R. Nathan and Mrs. Nathan (9–16 May 2009)

In May 2009, the late President S. R. Nathan and Mrs. Nathan made the first State Visit to Japan at the invitation of Emperor Akihito and Empress Michiko.

In 2003, Japan had offered an official visit to our President. An official visit, unlike a state visit, would include only a call on the Emperor and a lunch to be hosted by him but no hospitality. Gaimusho and Kunai-chō had very rigid rules as to who and which country could be invited to a state visit. Happily, the June 2006 State Visit by the Emperor and Empress to Singapore opened the way for Japan to invite our President for a reciprocal state visit. In 2008, we received hints from key officials of Gaimusho and Kunai-chō that they were planning to invite our President to a state visit. In 2009, this first-ever visit to Japan by a Singapore President took place. Hospitality included accommodation at Akasaka Palace, the State Guesthouse in Tokyo, and the Imperial Guesthouse in Kyoto. There was a ceremonial welcome at the Imperial Palace at which the President was received by the Emperor, members of the Imperial family and the Japanese Prime Minister. The Emperor also hosted a state banquet. At our request, the visit also included President Nathan paying respects at the Hiroshima Peace Memorial[4] and meeting the surviving victims of the 1945 atomic bomb. This gesture was appreciated by our Japanese hosts.

The success of the visit to Hiroshima was in no small part due to the efforts of the Hiroshima–Singapore Friendship Association Chairman,

---

[4]The Hiroshima Peace Memorial or Atomic Bomb Dome is part of the Hiroshima Peace Memorial Park in Hiroshima. Designated as a UNESCO World Heritage Site in 1996, it is a memorial to over 70,000 people who were killed instantly, and another 70,000 who suffered fatal injuries from the radiation of the atomic bombing of Hiroshima on 6 August 1945.

Mr. Eji Tamura, who was also adviser of the Hiroshima Shinkin Bank. He mustered the Association's resources and goodwill to support us during this part of the State Visit.

11 March 2011: The Great Tōhoku Earthquake and Tsunami

The Great Tōhoku Earthquake and Tsunami on 11 March 2011 caused widespread destruction of homes, workplaces and schools. More than 19,000 lives were lost, and one nuclear power plant in Fukushima Prefecture was severely damaged, causing radiation fears. Chew Tai Soo, Ambassador-at-Large and my predecessor as Ambassador to Japan, was appointed to oversee fundraising in Singapore for rehabilitation projects in Japan. The Singapore Red Cross raised a record S$35.7 million (~300 million yen) for rehabilitation projects in the Tōhoku region. Laurence Bay, my Deputy, led the Embassy's effort to persuade prefectorial authorities to work with the Singapore Red Cross on various community projects. Iwate Prefecture Governor Takuya Tasso, who was keen to export Iwate's excellent agricultural products to Singapore, was the first to sign a memorandum of understanding on rehabilitation projects with us. Other prefectures followed. Plans were drawn up for a multi-purpose community hall in Rikuzentakata City, a support centre in Miyako City in Iwate Prefecture, a nursery school in Shichigahama City in Miyagi Prefecture and a community centre in Soma City in Fukushima Prefecture.[5] These projects will sustain goodwill for Singapore in the Tōhoku region well into the future.

Looking after Singaporeans during the 11 March Triple Disaster

The Tōhoku triple disaster showcased another important aspect of the Embassy's work: assisting overseas Singaporeans in an emergency. At that time, several thousand Singaporeans were registered as residents and

---

[5] The Rikuzentakata Multi-Purpose Hall was completed and opened in 2015. Designed by well-known Japanese architect Paul Noritaka Tange, it includes a Singapore Hall seating over 300 people.

tourists in Japan. As railroad and air links were cut, embassy staff, including colleagues from our agencies based in Tokyo, such as the Economic Development Board (EDB), International Enterprise Singapore (IES) and STB, worked round-the-clock manning phone-lines to give assistance or advice to them. We worked with Singapore Airlines (SIA) to evacuate Singaporeans out of Japan when flights were resumed.

A handful of Singaporeans was stranded in the rural towns in the Tōhoku region, which had been declared an exclusion area due to fear of radiation. Fortunately, with assistance from the local authorities, all our nationals were evacuated.

The Singapore Civil Defence Force (SCDF) with their own rescue dogs were among the first foreign emergency response teams to arrive in Japan. They were assigned to a location some 40 kilometres from the damaged nuclear reactor. Their mission accomplished, they had to be evacuated quickly because of radiation fears. First Secretary Khoo Seow Fong worked closely with local military units and Thai embassy colleagues who were in the area to extricate our SCDF team to safety.

Nurturing, Refreshing and Renewing Familiar Ties

I regularly called on chairmen and chief executive officers (CEOs) of Japanese multinational corporations (MNCs) and small and medium-sized enterprises (SMes) (Hitachi, Sumitomo Chemical, Mitsui Chemical, Panasonic, Mitsubishi Chemical and other SMEs) in Tokyo, Osaka and Nagoya in the Kansai region. I would be accompanied by our EDB officers based in Japan.

These meetings enabled me to get from these top executives of Japan's leading companies a reading of the industry situation, exchange views or just to express goodwill and appreciation for their companies' support. They also provided an opportunity for our EDB officials based in Tokyo or Osaka to have a chance to meet these high-ranking Japanese executives. On their own, their access would have been limited to middle-ranking officials.

The chairmen and CEOs reciprocated my calls with invitations to lunches and dinners at their company guesthouses (kaikan). We made it a point to invite them to our residences for meals and on important Singapore occasions.

Some business leaders became personal friends. One was the late Mr. Hiromasa Yonekura, Chairman of Sumitomo Chemical and later Chairman of Keidanren, the all-powerful Japanese Business Federation. He was in the pioneer team of executives who helped start the company's chemical plant in Jurong Island. He joked that he learnt his English in Singapore interacting with our first-generation civil servants like the late Ngiam Tong Dow and J. Y. Pillay. Yonekura later became Chairman of Keidanren (Japan Business Federation). For his contributions, the Singapore government made him an honorary Singapore citizen.

Another friend was Egawa. He was a former Managing Director of Konica Corporation. Mr. George Yeo, former Foreign Minister, introduced me to him. They had served together on the Advisory Council Meeting of the Asia–Australia Institute at the University of New South Wales and had become close friends. As a young executive with Minebea and Konica Corporation in the 1970s, Egawa had visited Singapore many times during our early industrialisation efforts. In 2007, he donated his lifelong collection of Chinese and Japanese-inspired European ceramics to the Asian Civilisations Museum. Between 2007 and 2018, he donated his entire collection of antiquarian books, historic paintings and calligraphy to ISEAS Yusof-Ishak Library and the National Library.

The late Minister Mentor (MM) Lee Kuan Yew visited Japan annually, often in conjunction with his participation at Nikkei's Annual International Conference on the Future of Asia. His visits were opportunities to meet and exchange views with Japanese political and business leaders. As he often coupled his visits to Japan with one to China, his insights into the regional situation were valued by the Japanese.

As Ambassador, I had the rare opportunity to be in such meetings. On one occasion, just before PM Koizumi was about to step down, a Japanese leader who was involved in deliberations on leadership succession asked MM Lee how he selected leaders. MM Lee gave his reply by way of an anecdote. He recounted that while on a visit to a New Zealand sheep farm, he observed that the shepherd, using a lead dog, was able to control hundreds of grazing sheep. He asked the farmer how he selected the lead dog. The farmer replied that "when he was looked deeply into the eyes of a dog he instinctively knew if he would make a leader". This resonated with the Japanese leader.

An Ambassador's Wife Complements His Work

An ambassador's spouse can provide important support for his work. Japan had many organisations whose members were wives of prominent businessmen or political leaders. The prominent ones included Nadeshiko-kai, Asia-Pacific Ladies Friendship Society (ALFS) and the International Ladies Benevolent Society (ILBS). Their patrons were members of the Imperial family or prominent political leaders. They provided a ready platform for my spouse and me to build relationships with them and their spouses, facilitating my work as a diplomat.

Maintaining Political Links in a Fluid Situation

From 2006 to 2012, Japan experienced a quick succession of prime ministers, beginning with the LDP's Shinzō Abe, Yasuo Fukuda and Tarō Asō. The Democratic Party of Japan (DPJ) which took power in 2009 had Yukio Hatoyama, then Naoto Kan and finally Yoshihiko Noda. As all of them served a year or less on the job, maintaining close bilateral relations at the highest political level was challenging. Exchange political visits were infrequent. While trying to build links with the new DPJ governing officials, we continued to maintain close contact with LDP, including inviting their key members to meet visiting Singapore political officeholders. The DPJ's rule was short-lived and the LDP returned to power in December 2012 with PM Abe as PM for a second term.

Conclusion

Japanese culture, creativity, meticulousness, inventiveness and the industry of its people deeply impressed me. Their cohesiveness and resilience when under severely adverse conditions during the Tōhoku triple disasters, earthquake, tsunami and radiation in March 2011 were an example to the world.

I left Japan at the end of January 2012.

A Diplomatic Crisis

by R. Raj Kumar

There are occasions when a Foreign Service Officer posted abroad must handle a crisis. I was the Charge d'Affaires at the Singapore Embassy in the Philippines in 1995 when intense public outrage against the Singapore government was sparked after our Courts handed a death sentence to Flor Contemplacion, a Filipino domestic helper in Singapore. She was found guilty of killing two people — Delia Maga, another Filipino maid, and Nicholas Huang (aged 4), the child of Maga's employer. Demonstrations were staged outside the Singapore Embassy; Singapore flags were burned and the Embassy received bomb threats. According to Professor S. Jayakumar, who was Singapore's Foreign Minister at that time, this episode was a major diplomatic crisis and brought Singapore and the Philippines to the brink of severing diplomatic relations.

Anti-Singapore sentiments ran high following weeks of local media reports sensationalising the Contemplacion case. She was portrayed as a poor migrant worker who was a victim of a miscarriage of justice. As many Filipinas worked abroad, this struck an emotional chord with the public. Initially, the demonstrations outside the Singapore Embassy were peaceful, with the crowd numbering in the tens, but within a week it had swelled to hundreds. At its height, there were about 1,200 demonstrators outside the Embassy. The demonstrators also became increasingly aggressive and on one occasion attempted to climb over the Embassy's wall to pull down the Singapore flag. Fearing for their safety, Singaporeans who were in the country on holiday or business cut short their visit. There were a number of Singaporeans who worked in Manila and had their families with them. Our Embassy contacted them and mobilised our contacts through the Singapore Club to advise that they should return to Singapore with their families. The Ministry of Defence (MINDEF) also worked quickly to defuse a potential flashpoint. At that time, our armed forces were having their regular joint training with their Philippine counterparts. It was reported that some Filipino soldiers had expressed anger over the news that Contemplacion was being sentenced to death. The joint training was cut short and our troops were brought home quickly.

With the crisis deepening, the Ministry of Foreign Affairs (MFA) instructed the return of non-essential embassy staff including spouses and children. For the latter, this meant disruption to their schooling. A few days after the execution of Contemplacion, bilateral relations took a sharp downturn with the Philippines recalling its Ambassador to Singapore and downgrading its diplomatic representation to Charge d'Affaires. Singapore responded by recalling our Ambassador to the Philippines. The visit to Manila by then Prime Minister Goh Chok Tong and the scheduled joint naval exercises were also postponed.

As Charge d'Affaires, I was Singapore's point person on the ground during this delicate period. Fortunately, there were clear-headed people in the Philippine Department of Foreign Affairs led by then Secretary of Foreign Affairs Robert Romulo and later the late Secretary Domingo Siazon. Foreign Minister Jayakumar kept in contact with them and I assisted by providing daily ground assessments and passing sensitive messages through Evan Garcia, staff officer to Romulo. Evan and I met up frequently and worked behind the scenes to help calm the situation.

The security situation worsened in the days following the execution. Filipino anger against Singapore was palpable and was exploited by opposition politicians, non-governmental organisations (NGOs) and the freewheeling media in the run up to the May 1995 general elections. It was during this time that two events happened which triggered MFA to step up security. One, we began receiving bomb threats. We took the first phone call seriously and called in a bomb squad to do a sweep. It turned out to be a hoax, but such calls continued over the next few days. Two, as representative of the Singapore government, I was targeted. On one of the days during this period, when I was on my way to the Embassy, my driver noticed a car following us. I instructed the driver not to drop me at the

A Diplomatic Crisis

entrance, as he would normally do (our Embassy at that time was in an office complex) but to go in by the back entrance through the garage which had a shuttered gate. As soon as the gate was dropped, we heard tires screech, followed by loud banging on the other side. I reported this to MFA Headquarters (HQ) and very soon after, received instructions for all the remaining Singapore staff (four of us) to move to the Ambassador's residence and work from there. The residence was unoccupied following the recall of the Ambassador and it was safer there as it was located within a gated community.

Security was tightened considerably. Singapore sent over a team to assess the physical security of the Ambassador's residence and it resulted in the hiring of more security guards, boarding up of all the glass doors on the lower level of the residence, briefing on emergency evacuation plans and strict instructions not to go out unless necessary. We had a local maid who did the marketing and cooked meals for us. We lived in a gilded cage for about three months. As Chargé d'Affaires, I was provided with two personal bodyguards who accompanied me on my trips to the Department of Foreign Affairs. I was also told to wear a bulletproof vest on my trips, which I promptly disregarded as it was heavy and cumbersome. The focus during this period was providing HQ with regular assessments on Filipino reaction and coordinating with the Philippines Department of Foreign Affairs on its behind-the-scenes efforts with Singapore to defuse the situation.

By this time, public anger had turned against the Philippine government for not doing enough to protect the interests of overseas Filipinos and for neglecting to save Contemplacion's life. President Ramos' administration was under siege. He could not ignore the visceral public reaction. Ramos threatened to sever diplomatic ties with Singapore if the special commission he had created were to find that Contemplacion had been the victim of injustice. The commission's report added fuel to the fire with its conclusion that Contemplacion might have been innocent as their investigation allegedly indicated that she could not have killed Maga (one of the two victims). The conclusion by the Philippine National Bureau of Investigation was based on the examination of the exhumed bones of Maga (which had been repatriated to the Philippines). Singapore rejected the findings but agreed to conduct joint autopsies on her remains. Two autopsies later, including one by an independent international panel, the Philippine government finally accepted the original findings of Singapore's pathologists, and thus began the process of reconciliation between the two countries.

Looking back on my diplomatic career, my most challenging assignment was heading the Singapore Embassy in Manila during the Contemplacion crisis. It was a steep learning curve and highly stressful at times. However, it taught me the importance of keeping a cool head and focusing on the task at hand. It certainly helped that I had an excellent team of colleagues at the Embassy and that we worked well together. Singapore's quick action on the security front — warning our citizens in Manila, cutting short our joint training and stepping up security for the Embassy staff — played an important part in averting a potentially dangerous situation and perhaps even saved lives.

Reflections on My Career in the Foreign Service

by Robert Chua

I have been blessed in my 40-year career in the Singapore Foreign Service. I met mentors and worked with colleagues as comrades to defend Singapore's interests in crisis management and build strong bilateral relations with the great powers, Association of Southeast Asian Nations (ASEAN) neighbours, the United Nations (UN) and international organisations. Our goal was to anchor Singapore's survival as a small nation state. There are three episodes on the lows and highs of my diplomatic experiences.

1988: Washington Posting

I started my first overseas posting at the Singapore Embassy in Washington, D.C. in March 1987. Under the inspirational leadership of Ambassador Tommy Koh, the Embassy had an excellent team of Singaporean diplomats and local staff. This was the era of a confident America under the late President Ronald Reagan. I learned from Ambassador Koh how to cultivate friendly and cooperative ties with the United States (US) government, Congress, think-tanks and the media to promote Singapore as a reliable friend in Asia. A productive outcome was the successful working visit of the late Prime Minister (PM) Lee Kuan Yew who met President Reagan and emerging new leaders like the late National Security Adviser General Colin Powell in April 1988.

This learning journey plunged into shock a month later when the Singapore government requested that First Secretary (Political) E. Mason

"Hank" Hendrickson of the US Embassy in Singapore be withdrawn. In diplomatic practice, this request for withdrawal was a step lower than harsh expulsion under the term "persona non grata". Diplomats are observers in their host country and should not interfere in its domestic politics. Article 41 of the 1961 Vienna Convention on Diplomatic Relations, which is a platform for diplomatic relations between independent countries, states: "Without prejudice to their privileges and immunities, it is the duty of all persons enjoying such privileges and immunities to respect the laws and regulations of the receiving State. They also have a duty not to interfere in the internal affairs of that State."

The Singapore government statement said that First Secretary Hendrickson had urged several Singapore lawyers to contest the 1988 general elections against the ruling party. The US government's response was that it would recall First Secretary Hendrickson, but it did not accept the basis for the withdrawal request. When the Singapore Embassy received the news, I told Ambassador Koh that it was likely that there would be a tit-for-tat response by the US. He thought it was unlikely to happen given the good bilateral relations.

On 10 May 1988, when First Secretary Hendrickson left Singapore, the US State Department summoned Ambassador Koh. Assistant Secretary for East Asian and Pacific Affairs Gaston Sigur gave him an official note and said that it was with deep regret that the US government had to request my withdrawal (I was then First Secretary (Political) in the Embassy). In reply to Ambassador Koh's request, Sigur said that the US was not accusing me of any improper conduct but was simply retaliating against Singapore's action on the withdrawal of First Secretary Hendrickson.

State Department spokesman Charles Redman, at his regular press briefing, reiterated that the US had requested my withdrawal with regret. He added, "The US highly values its ties with Singapore, which we have regarded as among our strongest friends in East Asia.... (we) hope that we can now put this unfortunate episode behind us." Ambassador Koh explained to the press that I had done nothing wrong, and I had been asked to leave because of tit-for-tat by the US, as First Secretary Hendrickson and I were of the same rank.

To date, this remains the first publicly known case of a Singaporean diplomat who had been asked to leave his posting by the host country. Ambassador Koh was distraught upon returning to the Embassy as he told me about the US' request. Ever the caring boss, he offered to take my place. I said I would comply with the US' request following diplomatic practice. The State Department was gracious in giving me one week to pack up and leave. Friends from the Pentagon and Congress and diplomatic corps phoned to wish me well before my departure. I cried as I packed up at home and reflected on this bizarre event, which was the lowest point in my career.

Emotions were high in Singapore and the US over this diplomatic incident, which made front-page news. On 11 May 1988, over 4,000 unionists and workers attended a rally at the Singapore Conference Hall organised by the National Trades Union Congress to protest US interference in Singapore's domestic politics. In this context, my aim was to help to repair this diplomatic strain by keeping a low profile and not inflame tensions. I requested my Ministry of Foreign Affairs (MFA) colleagues not to welcome me home at Changi Airport with their plan of a lion dance. Instead, they helped me to arrive quietly and avoid the media. When I reported for work at MFA, I received a personally handwritten farewell letter from First Secretary Hendrickson which he airmailed upon his return to the US. I knew him and his wife Anne, who was also a diplomat in the US Embassy in Singapore, before my departure for my Washington posting.

With time, Singapore–US relations were mended. In June 2002, the US State Department allowed me to return to serve as Singapore's Consul-General in San Francisco, a signal that the US government had long moved on from the Hendrickson issue.

The sudden termination of my first overseas posting was what American author Jason Redman called a "life ambush" — an unexpected catastrophic event that leaves a permanent impact on your life or career. I managed the 1988 "life ambush" as best I could to preserve friendly and cooperative relations as the US is an important factor for Singapore's survival. Looking back today, Singapore–US relations are cordial, sound and longstanding. The "life ambush" of my Washington posting was a valuable lesson for me to be resilient and exercise our foreign policy principle of being a friend to many and enemy to none.

1989: Singapore's First Participation in a UN Peacekeeping Operation

On 29 March 1989, as Deputy Director in MFA's International Organisations Directorate, I received an urgent message from our Permanent Representative to the UN, Ambassador Chan Heng Chee. She reported that the late UN Secretary-General (UNSG) Javier Pérez de Cuéllar had urgently requested Singapore to send a police contingent to support the UN Transition Assistance Group (UNTAG) which was a peacekeeping force to oversee Namibia's transition to independence via UN-supervised elections. The Singapore government promptly agreed to his request. MFA and the Ministry of Home Affairs (MHA), with technical advice from the Defence Ministry scrambled to put together a 21-man police team as they were expected to be deployed within one month.

My Director Mr. Chan Heng Wing and I worked closely with MHA Director of Manpower Mr. Alan Chan and Police Deputy Superintendent Mr. Lum Hon Fye, who made a recce trip to Namibia in southwest Africa, to pick the 21 police officers among volunteers with operational experiences and high physical fitness and prepared the logistics for their deployment.

Led by Acting Superintendent Mr. Lee Kok Leong, they had a three-week training course to acclimatise to Namibia's desert conditions and exposure to high-security risks. The driest country in Sub-Saharan Africa, Namibia is 1,144 times the size of Singapore but with a population of only 2 million. With uncertain medical facilities on the ground, our police officers were picked with the same blood groups for prompt blood transfusions to each other in the event of a medical emergency. From their 5 May 1989 deployment in Namibia's capital Windhoek and four towns, our contingent went on daily bush patrols lasting as long as eight hours over vast distances and extreme weather, settling communal disputes, inspecting refugee camps, and guarding and escorting registration papers for the upcoming elections.

In September 1989, Police Deputy Superintendent Lum and I visited our contingent who were deployed in the five towns in three-man and five-man teams. I was proud to see them in good health and high spirits. They were disciplined and skilled in their police duties which I saw in Katutura, a poor district that few contingents wanted to visit, given the high-security risks. Our police officers were well-received by the Namibians for the fair and impartial performance of their duties. The UNTAG Police Commissioner commended them highly for their dedication, initiative and professionalism.

In October 1989, the UNSG requested Singapore to send another 27 police officers, who were quickly deployed in Namibia after a one-week training course. Singapore also sent a 20-man team from the Elections Department to help in the UN-supervised free and fair elections in November 1989 which were held successfully for Namibia's independence. Namibia joined the UN on 23 April 1990 as its 160th member state. Our 48-member police contingent completed their 43 weeks of UNTAG duties and returned to Singapore in March 1990. They served with distinction and were awarded the UNSG's medal.

I will always fondly remember being part of the inter-ministry team that organised Singapore's first participation in a UN peacekeeping operation (UNPKO) with very short preparation time and little feel of the ground situation in Namibia as an unfamiliar operating environment in Africa. The lesson learned in our nimble foreign policy response is that Singapore has a "can-do" spirit in fulfilling our international responsibilities with a "whole-of-government" approach. This first successful UNPKO participation raised Singapore's standing in the UN as an effective and reliable member state and enhanced our friendship with Namibia and other African countries.

2008: Emergency Relief Work After Cyclone Nargis

I was shell-shocked that a huge Category 4 storm, Cyclone Nargis, came in from the Bay of Bengal and devastated the low-lying Ayeyarwady Delta and Yangon on 2 May 2008. It was Myanmar's worst natural disaster with a storm surge of 40 km up the densely populated Delta and peak destructive winds of 165 km/hour. Over 138,000 lives were lost, and the livelihoods of 2.4 million people severely affected with entire villages wiped out. The Delta areas comprised Myanmar's rice bowl and core of its fishing industry. Over 25,000 sq km were directly hit by the Cyclone. Over 40% of all food stocks and about 48% of the 7,257 schools were destroyed.

As Ambassador to Myanmar, I oversaw the crisis management of looking after the Singaporean community, repair of the damage to the Embassy and my residence. Back-up generators ran non-stop as there was no electricity for almost two weeks. I also coordinated with the Myanmar government to hand over at Yangon Airport the emergency humanitarian aid sent by the Singapore government. I was supported by my dedicated and diligent Singaporean and Burmese staff. The Singapore government also sent a Health Ministry medical team to help Myanmar in its emergency relief for the Cyclone Nargis survivors. Concurrently, medical teams from the Singapore Red Cross and Mercy Relief also arrived in Yangon to help. However, in the confused post-disaster situation of difficult local conditions and logistical challenges and with the host government overwhelmed, the deployment of the three medical teams was delayed and uncertain. I suggested to our Health Ministry to combine the three teams under a "Team Singapore" approach and then secured the Myanmar Health Minister's decision to deploy them in Twante township outside Yangon, where they treated about 5,000 cyclone victims from rural areas. It worked very well as all the team members had different talents and experiences that they gelled together as a professional medical team.

After their deployment, "Team Singapore" recommended to me to help a rural village named Kayin Chaung to complete their 16-bed community hospital so that the rural villagers would not have to travel nearly two hours to Yangon for medical treatment. The village committee ran out of funds in the construction phase. This 16-bed hospital was completed in nine months as the Singapore government's Cyclone Nargis recovery project to help the Myanmar people. Today, it is regarded as a model 16-bed community hospital by the Myanmar Health Ministry and is fondly called the "Singapore Hospital" by the rural hinterland of over 10,000 people.

The Singapore government also donated a set of ground handling equipment to the Myanmar government to help unload tons of international aid arriving daily at Yangon Airport. They were initially unloaded by many weary youth volunteers and uniformed personnel. I coordinated the delivery of the equipment and training of the airport staff by a technical team from Changi Airport to help them operate the equipment. Other Singapore government humanitarian aid that I planned and delivered was the donation of 1,000 fishing boats to help the affected fishermen in the

Ayeyarwady Delta to regain their livelihoods, the donation of 58,000 bags of fertiliser to help farmers save their July rice crop and the construction of over 250 tube wells to help rural villagers have drinking water during the yearly dry season.

As Singapore was then the ASEAN Chair, I was asked by MFA to represent ASEAN as its representative in the Myanmar–ASEAN–UN "Tripartite Core Group" (TCG) created by the ASEAN foreign ministers to help military-ruled Myanmar work with the international community to bring in relief aid, and international aid workers to support the massive emergency relief phase of search and rescue and aid distribution, and overcome its concerns of foreign interference. The TCG members from ASEAN and the UN called on our Chairman, Deputy Foreign Minister U Kyaw Thu at the Foreign Ministry in Yangon, on 31 May. I told my colleagues that the TCG was like a jazz band as much of our work was improvisation since such a tripartite mechanism had never been undertaken in international relations. We enjoyed good chemistry and had honest and frank discussions on doing as much as we could in the critical emergency relief phase. Our common aim was to save and rebuild the lives of the survivors. Deputy Foreign Minister Kyaw Thu trusted the ASEAN team as an honest broker and in the first month of the TCG's work, he asked me to stand-in and chair the TCG meeting for him whenever he was overseas on official duty. The UN colleagues also trusted me and my ASEAN colleagues.

One aspect of the emergency humanitarian work showed the trust ASEAN built in the TCG. Without satellite capabilities, the Myanmar government did not have any idea about the huge devastation caused by Cyclone Nargis. The only way was to send joint assessment teams comprising Myanmar, ASEAN and UN officials quickly by helicopters, boats and cars to the affected areas. In these massive joint efforts by the UN, ASEAN and the Myanmar government, I was capably supported by Colonel Kadir Maideen Mohamed and Major Ow Yong Tuck Wah of the Singapore Civil Defence Force. With their extensive experience in disaster management, they quickly set up the TCG 24-hour control room in Yangon to guide the 325-member joint assessment teams and record their feedback from ground zero. Major Ow jointly led a damage assessment team comprising Myanmar, ASEAN and UN officials to Labutta, the most devastated township in the affected areas.

The ASEAN embassies, in a collective show of solidarity, deployed their diplomatic staff to man the 24/7 control room until the joint assessment teams returned safely to Yangon from their two-week deployment. The UN also sent their Country Team agencies in Myanmar to support this exercise. The Myanmar government was significantly cooperative in facilitating unrestricted access to the affected areas and providing 50 portable sets of CDMA phones based on military communication technology with wide coverage from the Ayeyarwady Delta to Yangon for the joint assessment teams to communicate with the TCG control room. This historic joint field assessment involved about 350 persons from ASEAN, UN, World Bank, Asian Development Bank, local civil society volunteers and non-governmental organisations. The Myanmar government deployed 20 officers from 18 ministries.

I was greatly moved by this massive and united humanitarian teamwork. The TCG's damage assessment report gave the international community a clear picture of the urgent humanitarian needs in the Ayeyarwady Delta and subsequently formed the basis of the landmark Post-Nargis Joint Assessment (PONJA). PONJA was a credible joint rapid assessment of recovery needs and a shared recovery and reconstruction plan done by the TCG with the methodologies of the UN's Village Tract Assessment and the World Bank's Damage and Loss Assessment. It was submitted in time for the ASEAN Foreign Ministers' Meeting in July as a progress report.

ASEAN led and coordinated the international relief efforts through the TCG, bridging cooperation and building trust between the Myanmar government and the UN representing the international community. I believe the TCG experience opened mindsets throughout the Myanmar civil service towards international engagement as benefiting the country's development.

Myanmar was one of the first countries to recognise Singapore's independence in 1965. It was my last overseas posting and the highest personal satisfaction point in my Foreign Service career.

Doing Due Diligence for Singapore's "Excellence"

by Tan York Chor

At a ceremony in the Élysée Palace on 21 January 2011, then President Nicolas Sarkozy, turning to his then Foreign Minister Michèle Alliot-Marie, asked teasingly in French, "Et si nous invitons Singapour au G20 cette année... (what if we invite Singapore to the Group of Twenty (G20)[1] this year)?" Without hesitation, I said that it would be an honour for Singapore to work with France during its G20 Presidency. They smiled. At the brief reception which followed, I sought Sarkozy's then Diplomatic Adviser Jean-David Levitte's insight. He shared that France had just proposed to G20 its special guests, including Singapore.

Exceptionally held for just four ambassadors-designate, this credentials ceremony afforded a rare chance for a conversation, however brief, with President Sarkozy, an auspicious start to a very busy but fulfilling four-and-a-half years posting for me in Paris. Working with Singapore agencies, my team delivered Singapore's first-ever State Visits in 2014 to Portugal[2] and in 2015 to France by then President Tony Tan, while Prime Minister (PM)

---

[1] The G20 is an international forum of 20 major economies that collectively account for about 90% of the global economy, 80% of world trade and two-thirds of the world's population. The 20 member economies are the European Union as a whole but also France, Germany, Italy and the United Kingdom as members in their own right; United States, Canada, Mexico, Argentina, Brazil, South Africa, China, India, Indonesia, Japan, Republic of Korea, Australia, Russia, Saudi Arabia and Turkey.

[2] Portugal, to which I was concurrently accredited from Paris, appreciated Singapore's friendship during a difficult period of economic crisis.

Lee Hsien Loong visited France twice — for the G20 Cannes Summit in November 2011 and an official visit to France in October 2013. There was also a constant flow of working visits by then Deputy PMs (DPMs) Teo Chee Hean and Tharman Shanmugaratnam, and other senior people for bilateral engagements or key international meetings held in France.

Singapore's success and its diverse leadership roles at various international fora — in particular, the Global Governance Group (3G)[3] that Singapore initiated in 2009 for small- and medium-sized countries to engage the G20 — had helped position Singapore into a "sweet spot" when G20 hosts consider who to invite as guests to the G20 process. It also helped that some top French officials had, over the years, developed great respect for Singapore working with distinguished leaders — who believed in making friends — like our first Ambassador in Paris, David Marshall, and strategic thinker Peter Ho in his successive capacities. One of them was Levitte, another then Secretary-General of France's foreign ministry, Pierre Sellal.

France, in inviting Singapore, recognised our 3G convenor role. The 3G had hitherto limited its role to New York and somewhat less so in Geneva, where 3G members met to form their views and recommendations on United Nations (UN) and international issues on the G20's agenda, before putting these 3G positions to the G20. When fellow 3G Ambassadors in Paris wanted the 3G to meet French senior officials leading specific 3G tracks, I readily obliged, despite knowing that to request, arrange and chair these meetings would add a toll on our small Embassy staff on top of our regular bilateral work. One must do justice to those who put their trust in us by doing due diligence and acting honourably. Our 3G meetings in Paris won us further respect from French officials and fellow 3G colleagues alike.

---

[3] 3G is an informal group of small- and medium-sized countries convened since July 2009 by Singapore, at the latter's initiative, with the aim of serving as a platform to address G20-related issues and for collectively engaging the G20 such as by presenting to the G20 the views of the 3G membership. Its 30 members are Bahamas, Bahrain, Barbados, Botswana, Brunei Darussalam, Chile, Costa Rica, Finland, Guatemala, Jamaica, Kuwait, Liechtenstein, Luxembourg, Malaysia, Monaco, Montenegro, New Zealand, Panama, Peru, Philippines, Qatar, Rwanda, San Marino, Senegal, Singapore, Slovenia, Switzerland, United Arab Emirates, Uruguay and Vietnam.

Fast forward to 19 October 2012, on PM Lee's Facebook page: "French PM Jean-Marc Ayrault decided that Singapore would be the first country outside Europe he would visit as PM. I was happy to sign a 'Joint Declaration on the Strategic Partnership between France and Singapore' with Ayrault last evening...." In fact, Ayrault's visit was *his first-ever official visit as PM to any country*. Singapore became France's strategic partner in Asia, and France our second strategic partner after the United States, with which Singapore had signed a strategic framework agreement in 2005. Throughout his visit, Ayrault kept lauding Singapore's "excellence". He even called on his compatriots to emulate our spirit of excellence. (The French media during his visit was, alas, only interested in his thoughts on developments in France.) How did Ayrault, just appointed as PM in June 2012 following the French Socialists' presidential and legislative elections victory, decide to visit Singapore and step-up relations to a new level?

Sensing, Strategising, Positioning and Making Friends

Our Embassy's close monitoring throughout 2011 of the political trends in France pointed to the growing possibility of a Socialist victory. We expended efforts to reach out to officials close to Socialist leaders to capture a mindshare, informing them about Singapore and its outsized bilateral scorecard with France. One day, I caught a passing mention that then Socialist presidential candidate François Hollande, if he won, had then Nantes Mayor Ayrault in mind as his PM. I reached out to Nantes to learn about this amazing city that had re-invented itself under Ayrault, who ran it well. Nantes received us warmly. Later, I learnt that my French counterpart in Singapore, hearing that Ayrault was breaking a journey in Singapore in 2011 between France and a third destination, took upon himself to receive the mayor, showed him around and briefed him on Singapore. Ayrault was apparently impressed. Our own Embassy's efforts to reach out to him and Nantes months before a yet uncertain Socialist victory, when few would have even heard of Ayrault, let alone known that he was slated to be PM if Hollande won, probably dovetailed with his positive views on Singapore and its "excellence".

Where is Singapore? Making Singapore Better Known in France

In 2019, "Where is Sri Lanka" was the most Googled question on any country. When I was studying in France from 1977 to 1983, rarely anyone knew Singapore. People variously thought Singapore was somewhere in a dozen places: India, China, Japan, Thailand, Malaysia, Indonesia — even Africa! Once, a post office clerk refused to mail a letter to my father unless I deleted "Republic of" from Singapore and added "Malaysia" to the mailing address. Finally, he wearingly produced a thick directory to prove me wrong, only to see Singapore listed in it as a country. Imagine my great dismay to see, when I graduated from my engineering grande école in 1983, on the certificate that the French Ministry of Education issued, my country printed as "Singapore (Malaysia)". I had to return the certificate for them to re-issue a correct one. Coming back 28 years later to France in 2011, general knowledge had significantly improved but many French people remained ignorant of Singapore. Hence, it was worthwhile trying to make Singapore better known.

Arising from my sharing about Singapore with influential French personalities whom I had met and reached out to, various societies/clubs invited me to speak on Singapore. I always obliged and surprised their members on how far Singapore had come in five decades against all odds, while re-inventing itself endlessly. It also surprised them how, despite being a small city state, Singapore ranked among France's top economic, research and security partners in Asia. (Such facts go unreported. Despite our efforts to engage the French media, they stick to the Western media's jaundiced and caricatured portrayal of Singapore which sullied our image.) In some of these circles, I was the only — or only other, besides the charming, intelligent and talented Montenegrin Irena Radović — Ambassador to be included at their events. Some contacts I made approved of my having navigated into these fora where one could meet certain personalities who were otherwise inaccessible. These platforms also facilitated my inviting selected guests to Singapore events that we would like to interest them, such as when we organised the "Singapore in France" Festivarts in 2015.

To Have Culture is to Exist — Putting Singapore on France's Mental Map

To the French, a culture equals existence. My first task following my arrival in Paris on 1 January 2011 was to see our Ba Ba Bling exhibition before it closed. It had captured the attention of visitors with the Peranakan culture. Three years later, when Singapore was considering where to hold a cultural festival of unprecedented scale as part of our 2015 celebrations of Singapore's 50th anniversary of independence, I put in a strong bid to hold it in France, pointing out that the French, who live and breathe culture, would appreciate such a festival the most, adding that it would far exceed Ba Ba Bling's impact and would, *par excellence*, place Singapore on France's mental map. Moreover, it was a fitting way to celebrate the 50th anniversary of France–Singapore relations.[4] Thus was born "Singapour en France: Les Festivarts" from March to July 2015.

Notwithstanding the low-key inauguration that we had to adopt as a mark of respect to our founding PM who passed away on 23 March 2015, just when the Festivarts was about to start, the event was an immense success. Thanks to the good cooperation of our French counterparts, the hard work of all our agency colleagues and the talents and invaluable contributions by the numerous artists and artistes, the Festivarts was well-received. All in, over 70 events took place in more than 20 French cities, reaching over 500,000 people, with 200,000 visiting the contemporary art and design exhibitions. The French, Singapore and international media featured the Festivarts in over 280 articles, marking a rare occasion when the French media reported on something Singaporean positively. I tried to show support to as many events as I could, and managed to catch 28 of them in Paris, Lyon and Toulouse, ranging from the history of Singapore's cinematography and cinema, concerts and dance to the 1,000 Singapore's exhibition at La Cité de l'Architecture. I had worked with Design Singapore since 2011 to bring that exhibition to Paris. The late Professor Roger Taillibert, possibly the world's greatest architect (with a legacy of

---

[4] France and Singapore established formal diplomatic relations on 18 September 1965.

hundreds of works) whom I had the privilege of knowing, helped open the door to La Cité.

State Visit to France by President Tony Tan, 17–23 May 2015

At the height of the landmark Festivarts came then President Tan's State Visit. It was the top highlight of my posting and took a series of well-strategised lobbying efforts mapped out in detail, endorsed by the Ministry of Foreign Affairs, the Prime Minister's Office (PMO) and Istana, and implemented successfully to secure France's agreement[5] to host this key visit to celebrate the 50th anniversary of bilateral relations. The visit saw a slew of agreements signed, including one on cybersecurity between the newly formed Cyber Security Agency (CSA) of Singapore[6] and its French counterpart. Amidst his busy schedule in France, which included key meetings and banquets with then President Hollande in the Élysée Palace, with then PM Manuel Valls at the Matignon Palace, with Senate President Gérard Larcher at the Senate Palace and with the Mayor of Paris Anne Hidalgo and then Mayor of Bordeaux and former PM Alain Juppé at their respective townhalls, President Tan made time to meet with a group of Singaporeans living in Paris, and to visit the Republic of Singapore Air Force 150 Squadron Advanced Jet Training detachment in Cazaux near Bordeaux. For Singaporeans in Paris, it was a particularly proud and moving moment to see Singapore flags flying for the first and only time ever at the iconic Place de la Concorde and along the entire Champs-Élysées Avenue.

Network and Open Doors

I lacked the luxury of graduating from France's Ecole Nationale d'Administration, with its alumni contacts spread in every French

---

[5] Our success in securing a State Visit surprised many in the diplomatic community, and led to earnest questions, especially from Association of Southeast Asian Nations colleagues, on how we did it.

[6] It was CSA's first-ever international agreement and paved the way for close and substantial cooperation in this field since then.

decision-making sphere. However, I made up for that by creatively and painstakingly finding ways to reach and know a select few key officials (whose support was vital to securing the State Visit) as well as making inroads into various fora for networking. Key to this was to be interested in, and interesting to, others. I made it a point for the C-suite of CAC40 companies (40 most significant stocks) to know me, at least by face. All but two of them eventually did. For PM's official visit, I knew all the invitees for PM's networking dinner (which the French media, acting on a leak, touted as the dinner of "Who's Who" in France), and was able, as they arrived, to warmly receive and introduce each of them to PM.

With my contacts and avenues, I was able to help the Economic Development Board (EDB) reach out in particular to key family-led businesses, planting some seeds for long-term results. Professor Taillibert brought me on one of his visits to Toulouse to meet his old friend, Pierre Fabre, of the cosmetics and anti-cancer drug company bearing his name. On another occasion, at an exclusive club lunch to which I was invited, I was fortuitously seated next to the head of another such family-owned company who, after warming up to me, agreed to my paying him a visit with my EDB colleague, when his staff had rebuffed EDB's approach. I also reached out to interests-specific fora, delivering keynote speeches on Singapore as an aeronautical hub, as a regional "control tower" and other advantageous areas for French entities. I successfully urged influential chambers and clubs to consider Singapore in their plans and linked them with Singapore entities. Given the role of ambassadors, if there is one piece of advice to agencies, it would be to keep our ambassadors informed about their proposals. This is because if our ambassadors are asked, their ignorance may signal that the proposals are unimportant.

Although operating in multilateral and bilateral settings is very different — and I am proud to have served as Permanent Representative to the UN in Geneva and to the International Atomic Energy Agency (IAEA)[7] in Vienna, and Ambassador to France and Portugal — it is ulti-

---

[7] The IAEA is an international organisation that seeks to promote the peaceful use of nuclear energy as well as international cooperation to safeguard against access to and the use of nuclear or radioactive materials for non-peaceful purposes such as by terrorists or in military weapons.

mately about due diligence: being proactive, to sense, strategise and seize opportunities to advance and safeguard Singapore's interests. I conclude by paraphrasing the following suited to this context:

> Opportunities help those who help themselves.
> Look, and seek, and you may find.
> Ask, and ask, and it may be given.
> Ring, and knock, and the door may open.

Working for Singapore's Strategic and Security Interests Abroad

by Christopher Cheang

As diplomats, our responsibilities include protecting and promoting Singapore's strategic and security interests in our host countries. The following are two examples of my contribution to that effort.

Protecting our Generalised System of Preferences Status in Europe

From 1983 to 1987, I served in the Singapore Embassy in Bonn, capital of the Federal Republic of Germany (FRG) or West Germany. The Ambassador, Mr. See Chak Mun, and I had to deal with a case that highlighted Singapore's need to preserve its Generalised System of Preferences (GSP) status in the European Economic Community (EEC), now known as the European Union (EU).[1]

GSP is a system through which developed countries provide preferential tariff treatment to goods imported from certain developing countries. Singapore was a beneficiary of the GSP. It was in our strategic economic interest in the early years of our independence to retain our GSP status.

---

[1] With the formation of the EU in 1993, the EEC was incorporated into the EU and renamed the European Community (EC).

Singapore then had been independent for less than two decades and to develop our economy further, still required preferential treatment for its exports to the developed world. Many investors, foreign and local, had established factories in Singapore with a view to exporting their products to the developed world as well as to our region and the Asia-Pacific in general. The GSP's relatively easy and low-cost access to the developed world's markets was a key consideration for investors when deciding to establish a presence or open a factory in Singapore.

The FRG was the largest economy in the EEC. Hence, it was crucial that the Embassy maintained close contacts with its officials, especially those in the Economics Ministry in charge of GSP, among other important issues.

While Ambassador See also had his higher level contacts in the various government bodies, I had to deal with those officials at the working level on a regular basis. As a young diplomat not even 30 years of age, it was my task to ensure that these contacts were not only regularly and consistently maintained, but also strengthened. To that end, I would meet these officials over lunch or dinner (in my residence) and at other events. My fluency in the German language combined with my gregarious, loquacious and extrovert nature helped me tremendously in my efforts to make, maintain and strengthen contacts with Germans from all walks of life; it also enabled me to disport myself in Bonn's social life.

Some time early into my assignment in Bonn, our Mission to the EEC in Brussels informed us that the EEC was considering imposing anti-dumping duties on a certain item exported to the EEC by a foreign non-EEC member country investor, whose factory in Singapore manufactured this product. My colleague in Brussels requested my help in discussing the issue with my German contacts in the Economics Ministry with a view to seeking and securing their support against the proposed EEC action.[2]

Armed with a set of talking points and a background paper from my Brussels colleague, I met my regular contact in the Ministry a few times and put forward our case. Ambassador See also met my contact's boss. Understandably, the German side couldn't make any commitment, one way or another. It certainly wasn't their intention to place me or

---

[2] Brussels was the headquarters of the EEC's institutions.

Ambassador See over a barrel. Of that I was convinced. Despite being the foremost country in the EEC with a strong voice, the FRG was but one of several member states in the EEC. We in the Embassy and I as the political officer couldn't do more than what we had already undertaken.

Matters came to a head when the top executive of the foreign company whose item was to be sanctioned with anti-dumping duties requested us to arrange a meeting with our German contacts, with a view to putting forward his company's case in person. Initially, my German contact, on being informed of the request by me, was not keen on meeting the executive. Thankfully, he relented, in response to my consistent and polite persuasion.

I arranged for this executive to meet the German official, his superior and other interested officials; Ambassador See and I were also present at the meeting. The executive received a polite hearing, but as expected, the Germans did not commit themselves to any position. However, we had done all we could, submitted our standpoint to the German side, amplified by the executive's own presentation of his company's position.

I can't recall whether the EEC finally imposed duties on the item concerned. However, of this I'm certain — the case helped strengthen Singapore's commitment to work long and hard to maintain and preserve its GSP status with the EEC. In that regard, we in Bonn provided whatever help we could to our colleagues in Brussels. They represented the frontline, so to speak, in our dealings with the EEC. I read later in a United Nations Conference on Trade and Development publication that the EC decided to withdraw GSP benefits from Singapore, Hong Kong and South Korea as of May 1998.

Purchasing Russian Weapons

After Bonn, my next foreign assignment was Moscow (1994–1997).

In the 1990s, post-Soviet Russia was no longer the Union of Soviet Socialist Republics (USSR) that had preached and supported world revolution. It no longer posed an ideological, political or military threat to many states, including Singapore, not only because it had forsaken Communism, but also due to the fact that its economy was in tatters.

However, despite its many challenges and problems, Russia's defence and military-related industries still produced top-quality weapons, although state subsidies to the sector had been vastly reduced, and revenues had declined, thanks to a shrunken military within Russia itself, the former Soviet republics, members of the erstwhile Soviet bloc and pro-Soviet states. These states were natural clients for Russian weapons, but they too were in dire economic straits. Hence, exports for cold, hard cash to countries outside the erstwhile Soviet bloc or pro-Soviet states was one answer to this challenge for Moscow.

Under those circumstances, we began to develop a defence relationship with post-Soviet Russia. Singapore's Defence Ministry issued a news release on 15 October 1997 announcing the acquisition of the IGLA, a surface-to-air missile system. The purchase even received attention from the Russian media — the *Kommersant Daily*, a business newspaper reported on this event, according to the 22 October 1997 edition of the Aerospace Daily and Defence Report. Singapore purchased the IGLA, in what was to be its first from post-Soviet Russia. The whole process — exploratory talks, negotiations, conclusion — began shortly before I assumed my assignment in 1994 and ended some time in 1997.

I was personally involved in the process. Apart from my job as First Secretary dealing with political and economic affairs, I was, for all practical purposes, the Military Attaché (as well as Trade and Cultural Attaché). Naturally, I had to work with our Defence Ministry on the purchase of this weapon. The Defence Ministry sent many of its technical and other experts to Moscow to meet officials of *Rosvoorouzhenie*, the then Russian state weapons agency in charge of exports/imports. It, in turn, sent its officials to Singapore for the same purpose. The intervals between their visits were also spent on many details related to the IGLA's purchase, such as terms and conditions as well as technical details of the system, all of which I had to handle, with guidance from our Defence Ministry.

It was an experience I treasured. Although challenging in terms of dealing with technical and other details, it provided me with valuable lessons in dealing with Russian officialdom in the persons of *Rosvoorouzhenie* officials. I must also say, in retrospect, that dealing with Russian officialdom was not as difficult as I had initially imagined. But that did not mean everything was plain sailing. One had to meet them several times to iron out what one would consider routine issues, but obviously this perception was not shared by them. There were occasions when I also thought they were dilly-dallying on this-or-that-issue because they didn't have the answers to our questions. In any case, both we and they were determined to conclude the whole process as it was in our mutual interest — in ours, as we could secure a good weapon and in theirs, as we could pay in cold, hard cash, unlike many countries which had had to secure a loan or pay in some form of barter, to secure Russian weapons.

The Kingdom and the Crown in the 21st Century

by Lawrence Anderson

When you fly over Saudi Arabia (KSA or the Kingdom), the thing that strikes you is the vast, barren landscape of sand dunes, rocks and undulating escarpments. That was my first impression as I descended into King Khalid International Airport to take up the post as Singapore's Ambassador to the Kingdom of Saudi Arabia on a languid afternoon in March 2013.

Coming from tropical green Singapore and with no prior experience of the Middle East, I was eager to understand the politics, nature and make-up of the Gulf area and impatient to explore its environs.[1] And what a wonderful journey it's been! After six-and-a-half years in this ultra-modern 21st-century desert oasis, I pen below some of my personal thoughts on the Kingdom's political economy, society and religion, foreign entanglements and Singapore–Saudi relations.

Political Economy

I am bullish about Saudi Arabia's prospects and what its bold leaders are trying to achieve. The Kingdom possesses immense wealth and ready

---

[1] The Singapore Embassy to the Kingdom of Saudi Arabia is based in Riyadh and has oversight of the Singapore Consulate-General in Jeddah. The Embassy is concurrently accredited to the Kingdom of Bahrain as well.

access to technology, labour and foreign talents to override its domestic challenges. Significantly, KSA has a dynamic leader in Mohammed bin Salman Al Saud (MBS) who, for all his excesses, has shown the energy and commitment to drive his far-sighted Vision 2030 reform process. From my chats with the Crown Prince and his close advisers, I found that they are acutely aware that KSA has little more than two decades to diversify the economy away from its current over-dependence on oil before fossil fuels are replaced by renewables that are affordable and easily accessible globally. By then, MBS would be only in his mid-50s, and he wants to ensure that the KSA of the future will remain an influential and prosperous regional player.

It is true that Saudi attempts at change and reform have been a painstaking process, having to account for powerful vested interests. But the Vision 2030 train has left the station. My guess is that KSA will muddle along and be sidetracked by megaprojects and regional conflicts, or face catastrophes like COVID-19, but the overall trajectory is decidedly forward. To strengthen the Kingdom's push for reform, MBS has brought into the government knowledgeable technocrats and experienced private sector persons who in their turn have embedded younger, capable, well-educated Saudis in the mid- and lower-level echelons of state and local governments. The Saudis have also invested heavily in downstream petrochemical and petroleum-related products, as well as renewables, notably solar and wind power capacity, and drawn up plans to build two nuclear power stations. As the world's top oil producer after the United States (US) with 17% of the world's proven oil reserves, KSA will continue to rely on its sizeable oil and mineral resources over the next decade. This is understandable, as it will enable the Saudis to embark on the crucial steps to reduce their dependence on fossil fuels without having to sacrifice the energy needed to power their more diversified economy and create the necessary jobs for the people in future.

I do not mean to underestimate the forces ranged against MBS and the Kingdom. Within, the greatest challenge is to change mindsets away from an embedded sense of entitlement and to move beyond what is still very much a rentier economy. There is also considerable unhappiness over some of MBS's more cavalier actions. But from what I gather, the threat to his position and reform efforts is remote. The instruments of authority and control, as well as the ability to dispense rich rewards and promotions, remain firmly in the hands of MBS and his father, King Salman. As for external enemies, so long as Saudi money can purchase US weapons and protection, MBS has his back covered. Results from the reforms will continue to be mixed, but even if the Saudis achieve only 40% of Vision 2030, it can be deemed a success.

Society and Religion

In my view, religion will continue to be a significant factor because it reinforces the legitimacy and political aspirations of the ruling family. Islam underscores the symbiotic relationship between Al Saud rule and the ultra-conservative practices of Wahhabism. I saw this evolve slowly under the late King Abdullah, but it has transformed completely under King Salman and MBS. While Islamic teachings in the Kingdom are still highly conservative, what is noticeable is that some of the traditionally strict Bedouin cultural practices, often mixed with the Islamic faith, have been drastically curbed.

Since 2017, the government and authorised clerics have been promoting a moderate form of Islam, instilling a more tolerant attitude towards the status of women, guardianship practices, gender mixing and social interaction with foreigners. This is a significant and necessary step if the leadership hopes to achieve its Vision 2030 agenda successfully. It goes beyond the surface changes of glitzy restaurants and malls, women driving and changes to their attire, but demands a sea change in mindsets of older Saudis who for 40 years and more have been raised on a daily dose of strict Wahhabi practices. People do not shed their deeply felt beliefs overnight and the Saudi leadership knows it must tread warily to win over not only the clerics, but also a society that is still largely conservative and tribal in outlook. One indicator will be if tolerance extends to allowing Christian churches and Jewish synagogues to open and preach publicly in the coming years.

Religion will continue to play a major role because the Saudi governing elite relies on Islam's extensive support infrastructure to reinforce their right to rule through the distribution of largesse, patronage, goods and services. Some regional countries will be less reliant on religion over time, but in my view, this will not be the case with KSA. The Saudis and their King lay claim to the two most holy places of Islamic worship[2] which all Muslims are directed by Allah to visit at least once in their lifetime, and they define the religion as a way of life for the Muslim *ummah*.[3] The considerable influence the Saudis wield in these two areas, coupled with their generous dispensation of funds abroad, has won them much influence throughout the Muslim world. This will carry on because it has proved effective and because religion increasingly has become the battleground for influence amongst the region's major powers — Saudi Arabia, Iran and Turkey.

Foreign Entanglements

The 40-year struggle between Sunni Saudi Arabia and Shia Iran remains at the centre of the struggle for dominance in the Middle East. Several of my close Saudi and Arab contacts have shared their concern over Iran's success in forging what they see as a hostile Shia crescent of encirclement comprising Lebanon, Syria, Iraq and Yemen. This coupled with Iran's courting of Hezbollah, Hamas, the Muslim Brotherhood and the Houthis amongst others to fight its proxy wars have greatly alarmed the Saudis and Arab allies. While a tactical accommodation between KSA and Iran is possible, a more lasting resolution to their historical enmity is not, so long as Saudi leaders retain their firm conviction that Iran is an existential threat and Iran's theocrats hold firmly to their belief that the active spread and conversion of the region to Shia Islam remain fundamental to the regime's raison d'étre.

Over the last decade, new players — the United Arab Emirates (UAE), Qatar, Turkey and Indonesia — have entered the fray. But I do not see any of them replacing the traditional heavyweights. The UAE and

---

[2] King Salman has inherited the mantle of Custodian of the Two Holy Mosques, namely Al-Masjid Al-Ḥarām (the Sacred Mosque) in Mecca and Al-Masjid An-Nabawī (the Prophet's Mosque) in Madinah, both of which are in the Hejaz region of the Arabian Peninsula.

[3] The ummah refers to the Muslim community of believers worldwide, united in their devotion to one God, Allah.

Qatar, despite their immense wealth and astute manoeuvring, are too small to dominate. Indonesia has the size and population numbers, but it is not Arab, a distinct disadvantage when even Southeast Asian Muslims believe that an Arab cleric is more respected and better qualified to preach than a local *Ustaz*.[4] Turkey's great advantage is that unlike Shia Iran, it is a Sunni Muslim state and therefore poses a direct challenge to Saudi claims to speak for the Muslim (Sunni) community worldwide. But Turkey is viewed with great suspicion by its Arab neighbours and President Recep Tayyip Erdoğan is seen as a latter-day Ottoman Sultan, bent on restoring the past glories of Empire.

As for the major powers, the US remains the prime influencer of events. But in exactly what way under the Biden Administration is the question asked by all the regional players. While America now is self-sufficient in its energy needs, I do not believe it will allow Saudi oil reserves or Qatari natural gas deposits to fall into the hands of Iran and Russia, or Islamist groups. Washington will not abandon its role as the guarantor of the sovereignty of its Gulf allies. What is of concern to the Saudis is whether this guarantee extends to the preservation of Al Saud rule. It is a legitimate concern given that Biden was vice-president when the Obama Administration was seen to have abandoned a staunch US ally, the late Egypt President Hosni Mubarak, during the 2011 Arab Spring. Another major concern is Biden's attempts to revive the Joint Comprehensive Plan of Action (JCPOA).[5] Whatever the outcome, the US will continue to exert its dominant influence, though not necessarily to dictate regional developments the way it wants.

China is not likely to challenge the US' position, provided Washington does not interfere with China's access to the wider Middle East and North Africa region's naval/port facilities, oil and mineral supplies. China's interests in the region are economic, oil and energy security. Even as its interests deepen, Beijing is astute enough to continue maintaining good relations with KSA and its allies on one side and Iran on the other. Chinese leaders have no desire to become embroiled in the region's quarrels. They

---

[4] A scholar trained in Islam and Islamic law.

[5] The JCPOA is the 2015 nuclear deal negotiated by the US, Iran, China, Russia, United Kingdom, France and Germany to place limits, safeguards and timelines on Iran's nuclear programme in exchange for the lifting of sanctions. Although repudiated later by then President Donald Trump, the Biden Administration is in talks to revive the deal.

are not so crazy as to commit military assets and risk coming into conflict with US forces for the sake of Russia, Iran or its proxies. Besides, the US and China have a common interest to maintain peace in the Gulf to ensure the safe passage of oil supplies and energy security.

Singapore–Saudi Arabia Relations

As the largest country in the Gulf and a major regional power, Saudi Arabia is of high importance to Singapore. Our economic interests are centred on energy resources, though bilateral trade is heavily in the Kingdom's favour. Singapore agencies and companies enjoy a reputation for honesty and reliability and are able to deliver on what we have promised.

My embassy colleagues and I have successfully leveraged Singapore's reputation. I will briefly cite three achievements. In 2013, after much lobbying of influential stakeholders and working in close concert with our trade and economic colleagues back home, we managed to persuade the Saudis to resume negotiations on the stalled Gulf Cooperation Council (GCC)–Singapore Free Trade Agreement (GSFTA). The Agreement entered into force on 1 September 2013 and Singapore became the first non-Middle East country to have an FTA with the GCC.

We also secured the Saudi invitation to attend the Group of Twenty (G20) Summit they hosted in November 2020.[6] This was significant, since Singapore is not a member of the G20 and to attend the prestigious event, an invitation must come from the host country. Our active lobbying began a year before the Saudis took over the Chair. We kept in close touch with the key Saudi agencies and personalities involved in the Summit's extensive preparations, offering useful suggestions and advice on topics and deliverables for the Summit. It was a whole-of-government approach involving inputs from our agencies in Singapore, even think tanks like the School of International Studies (RSIS). A critical factor were two visits by then Deputy Prime Minister (DPM) Tharman Shanmugaratnam, who was the Chairman of the G20 Eminent Persons Group on Global Financial Governance. Ably assisted by our Embassy, DPM Tharman met with

---

[6] Due to the COVID-19 pandemic, the Summit was eventually held online.

almost all the key Saudi leaders including MBS and even conducted a "tutorial" of sorts for senior officials on substantive topics for the Summit.

Beyond the handshakes, I cannot emphasise enough the value of having an embassy on the ground staffed by capable officers from the Ministry of Foreign Affairs and other agencies including Enterprise Singapore to look after Singapore's interests and the welfare of Singaporeans based in the Kingdom. Saudis, especially the influential business families, value the personal touch, preferring first to see if they can trust you before engaging in significant business deals. This is a major challenge to our government leaders and private sector chief executive officers given their busy schedules and the considerable distance and time to travel between Singapore and Saudi Arabia. So, it falls to the Embassy's officers to follow up on official initiatives or assist Singapore businesses in their efforts. This entails spending time meeting and socialising with prominent personalities, including their family members who often occupy senior positions in the family companies or government posts.

This is one of the job's enjoyable aspects, as the Saudis are excellent hosts in caring for their guests in their homes or excursions into the desert wilderness. There is nothing better to forge friendships than spending a day or two together racing over towering sand dunes, chatting in a desert tent in winter beside a raging fire, or watching Saudis proudly take their prized falcons through their paces and discussing the merits of their noble Arabian horses and contest-winning camels. I have had the privilege to enjoy these and other exciting experiences while making many friends in my journey through the Kingdom.

While personal friendships are important, I have also found Saudi business families and political elites to be shrewd and astute negotiators, whether it comes to assisting our visiting senior officials to conclude their negotiations or helping Singapore companies to link up and push through tough deals. We have even had to step in when our companies and their staff faced unwarranted intimidation and threats; fortunately, these have been sporadic.

I must stress that politics, economics, business and finance are not the only factors underpinning Singapore's interests with KSA. Of our population, 13% are Muslims, one of the largest percentages of a minority group in any country. During my stay from 2013 to 2019, close to

10,000 Singaporean Muslims annually made their *Hajj* or *Umrah* pilgrimage to Makkah and Madinah. I accompanied our ministers responsible for Muslim affairs and MUIS[7] officials to meetings with their Saudi counterparts to discuss, amongst other matters, an increase in the *Hajj* quota, so that more Singaporeans could make the pilgrimage.

We have over 200 Singaporeans working or studying in KSA and Bahrain and it is up to the Embassy in Riyadh and the Consulate-General in Jeddah to look after their welfare and safety. At times, this responsibility extends to Singaporeans based in neighbouring countries where we do not have any offices there. For instance, our Consulate-General staff helped to extricate to safety several Singaporean families trapped in Yemen when war broke out in 2015.

Conclusion: A Word on Information Gathering

The Kingdom is one of the most difficult places to gather good and reliable information. To influential Saudis, there is a distinction on what they are prepared to share with key allies — both Muslim and non-Muslim, Arab and non-Arab — and the rest. This explains why the diplomatic corps are so close in our interactions and consultation. For the Saudis and other "reliable sources", one is not always sure whether they are feeding you a line or simply recounting what they fervently hope will happen. In short, where the heart overrules the mind.

So, under these challenging conditions, how did the Singapore Embassy gain a reputation for being one of the more reliably informed in the Kingdom? In gathering, assessing and analysing information, I have relied on three criteria: VERIFY your sources to ascertain their reliability and biases; POSE questions and alternative scenarios, and DISCREETLY CHECK the information and hypotheses with other reliable contacts. This framework has served me well throughout my career. It is a rule-of-thumb I have endeavoured to instil in the younger officers I have worked with, including my colleagues in Riyadh and Jeddah, all of whom it has been my privilege to call friends.

---

[7] Majlis Ugama Islam Singapura (MUIS), also known as the Islamic Religious Council of Singapore.

Building Bridges to Brazil

by Tan Lian Choo

After independence in 1965, Singapore sought to establish diplomatic relations with most countries. In our early post-independence days, the Singapore Ambassador in Washington was concurrently accredited to serve as the Singapore Ambassador to Brazil, thus blazing the trail for our bilateral diplomatic relations with the Americas, North and South.

In 1985, then Singapore Ambassador in Washington Tommy Koh made the case to accredit a Non-Resident Ambassador (NRA) from Singapore to Brazil.[1] As a result, we were fortunate to have had the dedication and commitment of other pioneer Singaporeans after him, such as the late Ridzwan Dzafir, who became our first NRA to Brazil while he served concurrently as a senior official at the then Trade Development Board (TDB), and later Choo Chiau Beng from the corporate sector. Through regular visits to Brazil, first by the Washington-based ambassadors then by the Singapore-based NRAs, these early pioneering ambassadors paved the way for cordial Singapore–Brazil relations. Mr. Choo, who served for over 12 years as NRA to Brazil, even became the Dean of the Foreign Diplomatic Corps in Brazil as the longest serving accredited ambassador, albeit in absentia.

---

[1] Singapore's Washington-based Ambassadors to Brazil date back to 1967: Wong Lin Ken (1967–1968); E. S. Monteiro (1969–1976); P. Coomaraswamy (1976–1984); Tommy Koh (1984–1986).
Singapore's NRAs to Brazil were: Ridzwan Haji Dzafir (1986–1997); Lee Ying Cheun (1997–2000); Choo Chiau Beng (2004–2016). The present Singapore NRA to Brazil, Sam Goi, was appointed in 2018.

Assignment to Brazil

In 2012, upon the Singapore government's decision to open its first embassy in Latin America, I was entrusted by the Ministry of Foreign Affairs (MFA) with the task of setting up the Singapore Embassy in Brasilia, the capital of Brazil. I was to be Singapore's first Head of Mission, resident in Brasilia. I was to build upon the good relations that our past Washington-based ambassadors and Singapore-based NRAs had developed with Brazil.

I expected my three-year assignment as Charge d'Affaires to be very challenging, as the task of setting up a chancery from scratch was onerous. MFA then had no prior knowledge of work and living conditions there, and I was to lead a small team of three or four Singapore diplomats to break this new ground. Eventually, this experience made for a memorable one, both in my personal and professional life.

The decision to open an embassy in Brazil was in keeping with Singapore's need to expand its political and economic space to a part of the world where we had hitherto not established ourselves politically for the long term. Other Association of Southeast Asian Nations countries, namely Indonesia, Malaysia, Myanmar, Philippines, Thailand and Vietnam, had already set up their embassies in Brasilia.

Latin America consists of 33 countries (including the Caribbean), covering a vast tract of land that stretches from Mexico in Central America to Tierra del Fuego located at the southernmost tip of the South American continent. For most of modern history, Asia and Latin America were two continents operating in different spheres and on separate tracks. The long distance between the two continents, language differences, each with their respective colonial histories and post-World War II realities meant that each region coped with its own challenges, evolving its own systems of governance. At the same time, there were similar development challenges, such as alleviating mass poverty and raising standards of living.

By the early 2000s, however, Singapore was already open towards reaching out to Latin America. Efforts had been made to bridge the gap through the Forum of East Asia and Latin America (FEALAC), where member states' leaders could meet regularly and discuss mutually beneficial ways to enhance our respective engagements. On a region-to-region basis, Latin America and Asia had become more linked. Latin America's trade with Asia, especially with China, Japan and South Korea, had grown steadily. By then, Singapore was active enough to have a piece of this growing pie.

In the decade leading up to 2012, Brazil emerged as a substantive emerging economy. In 2011, it overtook the United Kingdom to become the world's sixth largest economy.[2] At least 55 Singapore companies were known then to do business with or in Brazil, while trade between Singapore and Brazil more than tripled in the decade between 2002 and 2012. Our economic agencies had identified Brazil for our engagement with Latin America, with opportunities for investment in oil and gas, urban infrastructure, trading of agri-commodities and manufacturing. Some 20 Brazilian companies were already based in Singapore at the time, some of them with significant regional headquarter functions. On our side, Enterprise Singapore (ESG), previously known as International Enterprise Singapore (IE Singapore), and before that TDB, had established in 2005 a trade office in São Paulo, Brazil's economic and financial centre. In 2009, the Economic Development Board (EDB) set up a regional office in São Paulo. Thus, it was that our flag followed the trade, and in 2012, the Singapore Embassy was set up in Brasilia.[3]

The Singapore Mission was warmly welcomed by the Brazilian Foreign Ministry, or Itamaraty, as it's often referred to locally, after the name of its famous building. Brazil has a long history of diplomacy and the Itamaraty is a distinguished institution. The republican state of Brazil was born in 1889, and the Itamaraty has since produced a corps of highly accomplished diplomats, many of whom compete at one of the country's most stringent

---

[2] In recent years, Brazil has suffered from severe economic recession, causing a significant contraction of its economy. In 2019, Brazil's gross domestic product (GDP) was ranked by the World Bank as the ninth (nominal) and eighth purchasing power parity (PPP)) largest in the world. With a GDP size of USD 1.847 trillion (nominal, 2019 estimate) and USD 3.481 trillion (PPP, 2019), it remains one of the world's most substantial economies.

[3] Singapore's sovereign fund global investment companies, Temasek and GIC, also have offices in Brazil. Temasek had opened its office in São Paulo well before the Singapore Embassy was established in Brasilia in 2012, while GIC opened its office in São Paulo on 1 April 2014.

entrance exams, known for its high levels of academic, intellectual and linguistic standards. Singaporean and Brazilian diplomats have often worked together at multilateral organisations, and we have enormous respect for each other. Our Brazilian counterparts are fluent in English, French and Spanish, besides their native Portuguese. Hence there may be little incentive among foreign diplomats in Brazil to learn the Portuguese language.

However, all Singapore diplomats serving overseas must make the effort to understand the culture and mores of their host country, and to do his or her best to learn the language of that country. It is difficult to be effective otherwise and serving in Brazil was no different. While Brazilian diplomats are often much at ease conversing in English, or any other major European language, other senior Brazilian officials often are not. As a Singapore diplomat, I was acutely aware that Brazil's most influential political office holders, whether at the state or federal level, often spoke only Portuguese. Theirs is the Lusophonic world, with its own rich offerings of literature and music — whether classical, modern or popular.

Therefore, I spent my first three months at intensive language classes, learning the Portuguese that is spoken in Brazil (different from that in Portugal) and soaking up all aspects of Brazilian popular culture.

Brazil's long history has seen its share of tumultuous economic and political upheavals. The contrast in our respective countries' history, geography and population size is certainly obvious from the way we work, live and perceive our relevance to the rest of the world — Brazil's population is over 200 million, its people united by a common language, largely isolated from the rest of the world in their day-to-day lives. Resilient and warm-hearted, the Brazilians I met always loved a good party, football and Formula 1 (F1) racing. Whether it was a taxi driver or an important Senator, everyone I met had heard of Singapore — they always saw Singapore as a beautiful city from watching the world's only night F1 race. The late Ayrton Senna, who died aged 34 at the San Marino Grand Prix in 1994, had become a legendary figure in the hearts and minds of the Brazilian people. Watching F1 races, like watching football matches, is a very common Brazilian pastime.

Their passion for football was also something I experienced firsthand. Brazilians are very passionate about winning over the allegiance of every newborn member of their family to become a fellow supporter of their chosen football club in the Brazilian premier league. When the World Cup was staged in 2014 in Brazil, the country's high hopes for victory by their national team on home soil were dashed so badly that even foreigners living there felt the national pain.

Sentiments, intricacies or nuances of the Brazilian culture and language held my interest throughout my stay. I could read the Brazilian newspapers without much difficulty. I already knew French and Spanish, and there are many common Latin roots in their vocabulary. Sometimes I found my brain translating four languages at the same time — from Portuguese to Spanish or French, and then English. Rather an unusual linguistic situation for a Singaporean to be in, you might say!

But there was much more than language and popular culture that had to be understood — the local laws were complex and complicated, and several obstacles had to be overcome for our diplomatic work to bear fruit.

Our pioneering team operated from a hotel room for the first year while searching for suitable premises to be rented, then refurbished as a Singapore chancery. Eventually, we succeeded — my colleagues and I truly felt much joy, satisfaction and pride (as well as relief!) when the Singapore Embassy was officially declared open on 5 April 2013 by then Foreign Minister K. Shanmugam. This official inauguration was attended by many influential Brazilian personalities, and the opening in Brasilia of Singapore's first Embassy in Latin America became a milestone event in the history of MFA.

Achievements on Assignment

At the time, Singaporeans still needed visas to visit Brazil. The first item on our political agenda therefore was to get the Visa Abolition Agreement ratified — this meant investing much time and energy, to explain and persuade Brazilian congressmen and senators, to support its legislative passage through two houses of elected representatives. This was a long and arduous endeavour, and even after that had been achieved, we still had to cultivate good political relations at all levels behind the scenes to see through to the final signature of approval by then President Dilma Rousseff. It would not have been possible without a diplomatic presence on the ground. Hence, it was gratifying to see our small team of Singapore diplomats, supported by our first generation of locally-recruited staff, achieve this and other important outcomes for broadening and strengthening bilateral relations.

There were many areas we started work on, from laying the groundwork for a bilateral agreement on the avoidance of double taxation (eventually signed in 2017), to ensuring that Brazilian food exports to Singapore met our agri-veterinary standards, e.g., for chicken and eggs produced in Brazil. Today, after experiencing first-hand COVID-19-related panic buying in our supermarkets, many Singaporeans understand better our national food security policy (which ensures a diversity of import sources) and appreciate how our government agencies and our diplomats abroad continue to work hard behind the scenes to implement this policy.

Successive teams of Singapore diplomats have since continued to work towards better Singapore–Brazil cooperation, strengthening our bilateral relations further. They have made much progress since our early days. Many Brazilians regard Singapore highly for its good governance and modernity. From the day we began our Embassy in Brasilia, we received many indications of interest from the federal government and select governors to learn from Singapore in the areas of education, public service transformation, water treatment, sewage disposal and public housing.

The pioneering team of Singapore diplomats in Brazil could not have achieved many positive outcomes without the kindness, understanding and cooperation of many others. They are too many to name here, including good Brazilian friends and fellow diplomats in the country, as well as our colleagues at MFA Headquarters in Singapore.

For me personally, I am grateful for the opportunity to have served Singapore's interests in Brazil from early 2012 to July 2015. The experience was particularly poignant when, at the passing of Mr. Lee Kuan Yew in March 2015, Brazilian officials and senior personalities, including senators who had become good friends of Singapore, expressed their sincere condolences. They had read Mr. Lee's memoirs,[4] visited Singapore and saw the achievements of our city-state.

---

[4] At the Singapore Embassy in 2014, we learnt that the Itamaraty had introduced as recommended reading for their induction programme of all new Brazilian diplomats the Portuguese translation of *The Singapore Story* and *From Third World to First*, the two-volume memoirs of Lee Kuan Yew.

One out-of-state Senator even flew specially to Brasilia to be there for just a couple of hours to sign our official book of condolences opened at the Singapore Embassy. Another influential Senator moved a motion of condolence at the Senate, speaking eloquently of the late Mr. Lee's contributions and inspiration. The Brazilian Senate rarely passed such motions for world leaders, having done so only to acknowledge the passing of great Latin American figures such as Che Guevara, the renowned guerrilla who became an icon of the Cuban revolution, and South Africa's Nelson Mandela. I was very moved when the Brazilian Senate recognised Mr. Lee and Singapore this way.

In conclusion, I can say that working for our national objective of expanding Singapore's political and economic space had literally taken me to the far side of our planet. I can also say that while I served abroad, the words of my late friend and mentor at MFA, Mr. Lee Chiong Giam, often rang true in my ears. He had an easy operational motto for our young diplomats as they went overseas: Be polite, patient, helpful ("PPH for short," he always said). I found this approach readily reciprocated in Brazil, as I made many friends that way, personally and for Singapore.

Rwanda — Mutual Cooperation from the Singapore Model

by Yatiman Yusof

Feeling Safe

On 21 January 2010, a day before I was scheduled to present my credentials to President Paul Kagame, I was shocked to learn that the senior lady accompanying me for my visit had completed her early morning jog. With the images of the horror of genocide still haunting my mind, I asked her why she risked her life jogging alone along the dark streets. She said that it was very safe in Kigali, and she felt good.

True enough, the streets in Kigali were not only safe, but they were also clean and motorists followed the traffic rules, a rarity in African cities. Rwanda was among the least corrupt, offering security for life and property. It was among the 15 fastest growing economies in the world, and a country that was well-known for its business friendliness and pride of its political stability, with 56% of its parliamentarians consisting of women.

Rwanda had managed to turn around the destructive Tutsi–Hutu animosity by building monuments with live recordings of the genocide around the country, surrounding the cabinet with majority Hutus, removing the ethnic references in the citizens' identity cards, rebalancing the ethnic representations in the country's security agencies, winning back the trust from among the diaspora of able and talented people who had left the country during the strife, reviewing its land policies, embarking on urbanisation in Kigali and spending 25% of the country's budget on education.

Meaningful Engagement

In the discussions of our diplomatic presence in East Africa, Kenya as a regional power that has been connected to us for some time remained high on our priority list. However, in looking for more meaningful engagements in Africa, Rwanda was seen as the obvious choice. Having openly declared that it wanted to be "the Singapore" of East Africa, I welcomed it as an expression of many things that we could do together.

Singapore was known among the African leaders in the 1960s as a member of the Newly Emerging Nations. The late Prime Minister Mr. Lee Kuan Yew worked hand in hand with the late Jomo Kenyatta, the late Kenneth Kaunda and the late Kwame Nkrumah, among others. After almost 50 years of low engagement with them, reconnecting it with the region was an important step in broadening our diplomatic base beyond the side meetings during the United Nations General Assembly.

The key to their success was to have a good leader in Paul Kagame. He is a brilliant ex-army leader who rules Rwanda with great commitment and tenacity. I was told that his reaction to corruption was swift, with any related complaints being dealt with within a week. His preference for using Singapore as a model for development was a big plus for us. By becoming partners in their development and with our experience in nation-building, we would indirectly leave a demonstrative effect on other countries to view Singapore favourably.

Capability Development Efforts

I knew that Rwandans were serious in their rebuilding efforts, despite being among the smallest nations in the world and a young independent country. If Rwanda chose to put aside the conventional path to economic development and opted for the development of infrastructure in communication, airports and opening the service sector and technology-based activities, we could help them achieve their objectives.

Rwanda was very keen on acquiring capability in creating effective management systems and the application of modern technologies. We started with working together in capacity building and developing human capital in areas where Singapore has proven experience. This included town planning, public housing, airport development and management, civil service system and technical education.

We arranged for technical training in the above areas. Where we could, we hosted visits of their officials here to study our airport management, air traffic control, urban planning, civil service training, public housing and workforce development. When they shifted from using French to English in their school's medium of instruction, we sent our education planners and English language teachers to Rwanda. Upon introducing technical education, similar assistance was extended. In wanting to develop their workforce, they modelled it against our Workforce Development Agency and garnered Singapore's assistance when developing their new airport in Kigali. Rwanda remains the most responsive country in taking up our offer for technical assistance, so determined were they to make the change towards achieving progress. And all these were to be achieved after a 100-day civil war and genocide that saw 800,000 of the country's Tutsis perish.

Laying the Path towards Connectivity

After facilitating a Singapore-assisted Internet planning session, I did a follow-up visit and was amazed to see thousands of workers digging trenches to lay cables along roads to connect outlying towns and population centres around the country. Within one year, the entire country was connected, and LCD boards were everywhere, for everyone!

One of my key interests in my work in East Africa was to establish a direct passenger flight connection with Singapore. We already had cargo connections with Nairobi via South Africa but passenger travel from here to East Africa takes between 19 and 21 hours. Connecting East Africa to Singapore will not only shorten the flight time to eight hours but will also open a new vista of links with the rest of Southeast Asia, East Asia and the Pacific with millions of passenger movements. Rwanda was among the first to offer Singapore Airlines a connection point, followed by Tanzania. However, it is only viable if the load factor is there, and it seems that Nairobi is the promising one.

Collective Advancement

Rwanda is a poor country. While several writers romantically refer to Rwanda as the "the land of thousand hills", when you travel through the country, you cannot miss seeing tragedy: adults and children returning from schools carrying water containers on their heads heading uphill to their houses, their lands rapidly fragmented and with families getting bigger and cultivated land becoming smaller, they can hardly produce enough food to sustain their families. With its per capita gross domestic product estimated at US$2,500 and per capita income of US$750 per year, the journey to elevate its standard of living is a long haul. Although its volcanic soils are indeed very fertile, water for agriculture is a big problem as the farmers rely entirely on seasonal rainfall and poverty alone prevents them from being able to manage the water effectively.

Despite the odds, I witnessed their tenacity in a unique project involving cooperation between the small tea planters and big estate owners within their shared "tea valley". They produced high-quality tea products, packed nicely as commonly shared brands and were marketed worldwide. Their agricultural exports consist of mainly coffee and tea and are available for purchase right here in Singapore. What started as collective marketing of the agricultural products amongst farmers has expanded into banking, adult learning and shared lighting for the entire village, all because of one man, a farmer, who had a dream of sharing what is good for the entire kampung.

Talents Return, Faith Restored

While many other countries undergoing political, economic and social upheaval saw a talent exodus of their people, in Rwanda, the reverse was happening. Many of its able citizens who left for the United States, Europe, Canada and other safer sanctuaries in Africa following the crises returned to help in its recovery. They were Rwandan diaspora who were exposed to the international economic environment, individuals who have acquired new technologies, wisdom and knowledge from international communities. They returned to apply their skills and capabilities. In working with them, I learned first-hand the value of love they place in their country. When asked, they said that they had faith in the new government and were prepared to give it a try.

An Encouraging Future for Bilateral Cooperation

I found my interaction with both members of the public as well as private interest groups in Rwanda encouraging and promising. They are quick to respond to our approaches, willing to talk about joint projects and keen on establishing multiple working groups. We were honoured to have received President Paul Kagame as the first leader from East Africa to visit Singapore in May 2008 and again in September 2015. The then Rwandan Foreign Minister Louise Mushikiwabo became our guest for our Africa High-Level Ministerial Exchange Visit in conjunction with the Singapore–Africa Business Conference.

In conclusion, I am encouraged by the level of bilateral cooperation that we have forged with Rwanda thus far. It is my hope that this could be taken to new heights in the years to come. Whatever we do, our key goals are to build a pool of support among our African friends in the international arena, create a community of partners on issues to protect and enhance our common interests and play a responsible role as a member of the world community.

My six-year engagement with Rwanda (2010–2016) was truly satisfying. Perhaps one day I will have the opportunity to return and finally get to pay a visit to my "cousins" (the silverback gorillas) up in the mountains.

THE FOREIGN SERVICE IN THE 21ST CENTURY

Three Projects in India — Navigating the Labyrinth

by Ajit Singh

Fifteen years of my four-decade-long career in Singapore's Foreign Service were spent in India. I deem it my distinct privilege to have served in all three of Singapore's Missions in India (New Delhi, Chennai and Mumbai). I spent more years in India than any other officer of Singapore's Foreign Service to date.

The time I spent in India saw rapid advances in economic engagement between the two countries. Singapore engaged in several mega-ventures in India that spanned years and presented unexpected hiccups and challenges along the way. I was involved in three such projects — the International Technology Park Bangalore (ITPB), the Singapore–India Special Economic Zone (SEZ), which later came to be called One Hub Chennai, and Bharat Mumbai Container Terminal (BMCT) by Port of Singapore Authority (PSA) at Jawaharlal Nehru Port Trust (JNPT) in Mumbai.

These projects followed an exhortation by then Prime Minister (PM) Goh Chok Tong to Singapore businessmen and companies to take advantage of the economic liberalisation measures initiated by then Indian PM Narasimha Rao. Mr. Goh clearly saw that liberalisation would provide fresh new opportunities and nurtured a special bond with Mr. Rao. This special connection saw Mr. Goh being invited to India as the chief guest at India's Republic Day celebrations in January 1994 where the two leaders signed a host of framework agreements.

It was clearly a turning point in the relationship between the two countries and one that has benefitted both. Prior to 1991, Singapore's investment in India was negligible and accounted for less than 1% of India's investment approvals. Owing to several bilateral initiatives, including the Comprehensive Economic Cooperation Agreement (CECA), Singapore is now the second largest foreign investor in India with cumulative investments amounting to US$115 billion across varied sectors including technology and logistic parks, warehousing, real estate, ports, hospitality, power generation and services. Singapore's trade with India has also increased more than tenfold between 1990 and 2021.

My presence in India during those years enabled me not only to identify opportunities for Singapore businesses but also to assist them in resolving their teething problems. That there would be challenges when doing business in India was expected. A business delegation to India in 1996 led by Mr. George Yeo, then Minister for Information and Communications, had concluded that while there was reason to be upbeat about prospects in India, there would also be a litany of problems and challenges those investors would have to face. Several of such challenges arose during the three Singapore projects and required the active involvement of our Missions.

International Technology Park Bangalore

This was the first of the three ventures that I was involved in during my stint in India. I took up my posting as Counselor and Deputy Head of Singapore's Mission in New Delhi in 2008 at a time when the construction of ITPB, which ultimately became Singapore's flagship project in India, was already in full swing. The project had the backing of both governments and the personal endorsement of both PMs.

The Singapore consortium for the project was led by Jurong Town Corporation (JTC). They partnered with the Karnataka government and Tata and Sons, India's most reputed company then headed by the well-known industrialist and philanthropist Ratan Tata. Singapore also had a very dynamic and well-connected High Commissioner (HC) in New

Three Projects in India — Navigating the Labyrinth

Delhi, Ong Keng Yong. For any rational observer, these circumstances should have translated into the smooth execution of Singapore's first mega project in India. Unfortunately, this was not to be the case.

The project ran into several hurdles during the construction stages and HC Ong did his best to resolve them as and when the problems surfaced. However, barely three months after I arrived in New Delhi, HC Ong was asked to return to Singapore to serve as the PM's Press Secretary. As the acting HC, the task of supporting the project on the diplomatic front fell to me.

One issue that cropped up was the delay in the construction of part of the road leading to ITPB. A wide, well-paved road was critical for the project. There was suspicion that a particular senior official in the state government was dragging his feet because he viewed ITPB as a rival to the state-owned Electric City, which was also under his charge.

I did not realise how upset the Singapore contingent was until I met a senior JTC executive over lunch during which he spoke about "exiting" and asked for my views on the likely fallout in such a scenario. Although he realised that exiting was not a serious option, it nonetheless helped underscore the point that the project was in danger of getting upended by the actions of a single bureaucrat. I assured him that our New Delhi Mission would leverage our contacts and help resolve the impasse.

Fortunately, HC Ong had introduced several of his good contacts to me before he left New Delhi. I also knew a Joint Secretary (Director-General level in Singapore) and Secretary (Permanent Secretary level) in the Indian Ministry of External Affairs from the time of my previous posting. I explained our predicament to them, and the Joint Secretary agreed to reach out to the Karnataka officer. They were batchmates from when they joined the Indian public service. She managed to convince the Karnataka official that ITPB would act as a magnet drawing global information technology players to Karnataka. Her timely intervention helped resolve the situation and prevented an inordinate delay.

What I gathered from that experience was the importance of close personal rapport with key bureaucrats at state and central levels in executing even a major bilateral project. The relationships that existed between bureaucrats who had trained together and had been subsequently posted all over India went a long way in resolving issues and problems.

One Hub Chennai

I was appointed the new Consul General to Chennai in 2006. I was specifically tasked to support the proposed Singapore–India SEZ — a bilateral project agreed between PM Goh and then Indian PM Manmohan Singh. This venture was intended as a model for India to follow while setting up SEZs and was meant to attract foreign investment, particularly from Japan that had only a small presence in India.

While I was comforted by the fact that the SEZ was a bilateral project and had the blessing of the central and state governments in India, I had no illusions that its completion would be without any stumbling blocks. It soon became clear that there were complex challenges that had to be resolved, many of which were interpersonal in nature. The resolution of these challenges required deft dealings with politicians, bureaucrats and vested interests at the state level.

The High-Level Steering Committee comprising of senior members from India and Singapore had little sway when it came to matters on the ground. Even the endorsement of the central government mattered little when it came to the single most important issue: finding a suitable parcel of land that was to be used for the project. India's SEZ rules at that time required 2,500 acres of contiguous land for the construction of a multipurpose SEZ. The acquisition of such a parcel of land proved to be a most difficult challenge.

On Singapore company Ascendas' suggestion, we first approached a key State Minister for state land. The Minister was supportive of the project but was unable to provide any state-owned land. He did, however, offer to assist with the purchase of land and to advise us on the complexities of land ownership in India. He ended up becoming our closest ally among all the ministers in Tamil Nadu.

What surprised us was that within days of my meeting with the minister, land brokers began calling the Mission to offer their services. Some even claimed that they had ready parcels that were immediately available. News of my discussion with the Minister had obviously been leaked. This resulted in a tricky situation as at least two brokers claimed that the Minister had suggested for them to contact me. Soon, other political players and civil servants got into the act. We brushed aside all unsolicited proposals while ensuring that we did not end up alienating any of our key supporters.

The land had to be bought at a competitive price which was only possible if confidentiality was maintained. However, ensuring confidentiality proved elusive as we had to turn to local officials for the arrangements. In at least one instance, a senior bureaucrat purchased a parcel of land from farmers after he found out that we were actively considering a particular area. He bought a small parcel which would have made it difficult for Ascendas to get a contiguous land parcel without buying him out. This was despite our best efforts to be discreet during our recce trips. We went to great lengths to remain circumspect and tactful during our land search. On one such occasion, in order to ensure that we were totally discreet, a Singapore minister had to walk a long distance through farmlands to check out a site because we had parked our vehicles a fair distance away from the landowners.

Faced with such unending challenges in securing a land parcel and after almost two years of searching, Ascendas decided instead to use a land aggregator to purchase land. Ascendas was able to do this at a margin. The difficulties faced by us in acquiring the land ended up delaying the project and significantly added to the cost of the project.

After the acquisition of the land, the next challenge was to obtain almost 30 statutory approvals. It took us almost 30 months to obtain the last approval relating to environment clearance. Regulatory requirements aside, there were turf issues involving departments within the state government. To resolve this, I spoke to the Chief Secretary, who happened to be a close friend of mine, and he agreed to chair a coordinating committee involving the relevant departmental heads. Although this helped to speed up most approvals, there were at least two departmental heads who were either overly zealous in protecting their authority or were unwilling to cooperate with the Chief Secretary for some other reasons. One of them even detested the Chief Secretary's involvement and suspected the Chief Secretary had a pecuniary interest, and another placed the blame for the delay on his minister.

A change in the state government following an election added further anxiety and uncertainty over the government's continued support for our project. Fortunately, the new Chief Minister was supportive when we informed her that the land had already been acquired. By then, the two difficult officials and the friendly Chief Secretary had been replaced. Despite the political and bureaucratic changes, bureaucratic challenges persisted. Thus, I used the pretext of a planned visit by PM Lee Hsien Loong (which did not materialise eventually) to set the wheels in motion for securing the remaining approvals. Meanwhile, the business environment in India changed and SEZs were no longer the flavour of the month. Ascendas decided instead to build an integrated township spanning 1,450 acres of land and is expected to be complete in 2022.

Bharat Mumbai Container Terminal

My final posting to India was in 2013 as Consul General in Mumbai. During my tenure, one interesting challenge I had to face was posed by an interested party that tried to prevent PSA from bidding to build and operate a container terminal on land owned by the JNPT. One party even contested PSA's eligibility to make a bid for the project in the Mumbai court.

While there were challenges during the construction stage, the issue relating to the employment of workers at the container terminal surfaced just before the commencement of operations. PSA had long-standing stipulations in place on the recruitment of personnel and awarding of tenders. However, some Indian political players and union leaders wanted PSA to bend its recruitment criteria.

Despite a complaint raised against me by a senior politician to a leading Singapore businessman alleging that I had failed to respond to his offers to help resolve PSA's problems with the locals, I took the position that PSA should stick to its established policies on recruitment and award of tenders. Protests by local groups linked to trade unions and political groups posed a safety issue for PSA's local management as some elements even resorted to violence and open threats. On one occasion, protesters blocked a senior management official from leaving his office. Under the circumstances, I approached the Chief Secretary and Director General of Police (DGP) of Maharashtra state, both of whom I knew and was confident that they would use their good offices to defuse the situation. My friends cautioned me that both the Chief Secretary and DGP could come under pressure from the politicians, but thankfully the situation was resolved. I was glad that we did not turn to those political leaders for help as that could have been another quagmire altogether. However, it was not an easy resolution.

Takeaways from My India Postings

As it turned out, my 15-year "baptism" into the dynamics of India's operating environment turned out to be a rewarding and satisfying experience.

There are huge opportunities for Singaporeans interested in doing business in India and, in my assessment, most Singapore companies are doing well in India. At the same time, the reality of the situation demands astute recognition of, and ability to deal with, a variety of challenges ranging from substantive infrastructure and regulatory matters to the bureaucracy political elites and well-connected businessmen. Undoubtedly, the situation is getting better. Successive governments since 1991 have undertaken economic reforms intended to improve the business environment and make India a more attractive investment destination. Current PM Narendra Modi's government has introduced welcome reforms, including labour and land policies, and has opened defence, aviation and insurance sectors to foreign investment. These moves have contributed to India being ranked 63 among 190 countries in the latest World Bank Ease of Doing Business Ranking — 70 notches up from 2014.

Doing business in India requires, among other things, close personal connections with individuals at different levels. Navigating Indian politics at local levels has unique challenges and Singapore's policy of engagement at various levels through its Missions has paid rich dividends. Singapore's success in finding proactive working partners within the state governments has been a key enabler for speedy and smooth implementation of projects. It is an oft-cited axiom that "all politics is local". Singapore's success in pursuing economic relations in India is largely attributable to excellent local networking and a good understanding of the ground issues.

Despite the challenges faced, I feel fortunate to have been a part of these three mega-ventures during my time in India. I would like to believe that I played a useful role in cementing Singapore's long-term relationship with India, and her businessmen and political leadership. My time in India continues to benefit me in my present role as a consultant with Enterprise Singapore to support Singaporeans desirous of doing business in India.

Singapore–New Zealand Air Talks: Off to a Flying Start

by Bernard Baker

In the mid-1980s, Singapore Airlines (SIA) was expanding its international routes and flight frequencies in keeping with the country's attempts to establish itself as a major tourist destination and aviation hub. We were also encouraging other national airlines to come into Singapore under what was mooted as an "open skies" policy, a concept well ahead of its time in a highly regulated and protected aviation industry. "Open skies" in its simplest terms just means that airlines should be allowed to fly anywhere they wish and pick and drop off passengers at all their stops if they want to do so. One can see the immediate advantage of such an aviation regime to a small country like Singapore with a limited population base.

To this day, all official Air Services Agreements have to be concluded between governments and not just airlines, although the airlines inform their respective governments and negotiators of their ambitions. Negotiating positions are then jointly decided upon between the airline and its respective government, notwithstanding the fact that the airline may or may not be a government entity.

In the latter half of the 1980s, I was the First Secretary and Deputy Head of Mission at the Singapore High Commission in Wellington. I was tasked to find out whether we could persuade the New Zealanders to come to the negotiating table, and if so, what we needed to do to expand our flight frequencies. We had learnt by this time that no amount of cajoling or pleading would budge the New Zealanders into air negotiations.

In fact, previous attempts to negotiate expanded frequencies had been blocked by a very powerful, and in those days highly protectionist, Air New Zealand. The airline was state-owned and influenced by its powerful unions, which in turn held tremendous sway over the Labour Party Government. If the unions did not get their way, they had no hesitation in going on strike, often costing the state heavily in political and economic terms. Despite these setbacks, SIA was determined to capitalise further on the lucrative Singapore–Auckland flight route, a task made more difficult then as the airline already had the lion's share of the market.

Armed with the briefs from SIA and the Ministry of Foreign Affairs (MFA), I strode into the office of a charming gentleman (whom for reasons of confidentiality I shall randomly call David). He was then the equivalent rank of our Director-General of the Civil Aviation Authority of Singapore. (David was later to become a friend who sadly passed away a couple of years ago after a heroic battle with cancer.) As with many New Zealanders, my contact was very open and frank with me. He said that it was unlikely that SIA would be given additional frequencies as Air New Zealand was struggling on the route in terms of its load factors. Secondly, SIA was a known great "6th Freedomer" which was resented not only by Air New Zealand but most of SIA's competitor airlines in those days. At this point I need to briefly explain the Freedoms of the air.

In essence, there were five official Freedoms in the 1980s (there are now nine recognised Freedoms if my memory serves correctly). First is the right to overfly another sovereign territory; second, the right to land in another territory for technical reasons like refuelling without the right to offload or pick up passengers; third, the right to deliver passengers from the carriers' country to another country; fourth, to collect passengers from another country and ferry them to the airline's own country; and fifth, the right to stop in another country and pick up passengers for onward travel to a third country. The "6th Freedom" was a dirty word in those days where an airline collects passengers from a certain country, stops off at its own home base then carries the same passengers on to a third country all on the same ticket. Nowadays almost all airlines fly 6th Freedom, and nothing is thought of it. In the 1980s, though, the aviation market was a very closed one and 6th Freedom was thought to be unfair and under-

Singapore–New Zealand Air Talks: Off to a Flying Start 139

handed. It was deemed to be not playing by the rules. To put it succinctly, New Zealand was worried that SIA would collect Kiwis, fly them to Singapore then on to the United Kingdom (UK) and other destinations, which would eat into Air New Zealand's market share even further, particularly on its lucrative UK market.

I asked David if he could suggest anything that would ease the fears of the New Zealand national carrier and at the same time placate the unions. He said that he would need time to see what could be done. I replied that I would wait to hear from him. Meanwhile, my next stop was to meet with a couple of the Air New Zealand unionists. I met with a chap called Charles (I forget his surname) who told me that "hell would freeze over" before the Airline's union would agree to additional rights for "that hard-nosed, bloody-minded airline of yours". At this point, I realised that it would be pointless pursuing the union route and decided that the next course of action should be political. I asked to see, and was granted an audience, with the then Transport Minister. The reader must understand that in most countries, diplomats have restricted access to ministers. New Zealand is an exception in extremis as Kiwis are very egalitarian, and their senior officials and ministers will usually see you if you have something useful to say or offer. This makes it the near-perfect environment for a diplomat to operate in.

Off I trotted to see the then Minister of Transport. I explained the situation to him with the most doleful look I could muster. I think I also may have told him that if there was no movement on our air services, I may not be given the opportunity to continue serving in his beautiful country. The minister chuckled, told me to hang tight, and added that he would see what he could do. A few days later, David asked to see me. We met in a bar and secreted ourselves in a corner out of view and earshot of the few patrons there.

David was a very decent human being and asked me what would happen to me if no agreement was reached to begin bilateral talks. Of course, the truth was that nothing drastic would happen and life would continue, but I simply reminded him that Singapore had capital punishment, without elaborating. David burst out laughing and told me confidentially that he was trying to work out something palatable to both the management and unions of Air New Zealand and that I should not worry. After several drinks, we made our way to our respective homes (in cabs of course!)

A few days thereafter, I received a call asking for a meeting with David. To cut a long story short, we worked out a deal (approved at home) that SIA could increase the number of its flights into Auckland once Air New Zealand's load factor reached 70% of SIA's on the Auckland–Singapore route. (This "triggering mechanism" was used later in other negotiations.) Another week passed before I met up with David and a few others from the transport ministry and unions. The Charles chap from the Air New Zealand Union was there looking very authoritative and less than pleased. David said that after much internal discussion it had been decided that it was possible to begin Air Service Agreement negotiations on an increase in flight frequencies based "on a formula that would ensure a fair amount of protection for Air New Zealand". However, he had to finalise the "fine print". I thanked him, knowing full well that our two sides would be soon heading to the negotiating table and reported back that there was a chance of a negotiated settlement if we stuck to the "triggering mechanism" formula. One or two bosses in MFA remained doubtful that we could reach a settlement, but SIA appeared to have more confidence in me, particularly my efforts in getting something positive on the aviation front. My then Permanent Secretary, who was later to become my High Commissioner, gave me the proverbial pat on the back for my efforts, even though nothing of any substance had been achieved yet.

A couple of days later, I again met up with David. We discussed our respective positions once more and he asked me if I was sure that SIA would go along with the 70% trigger. I reassured him that SIA would agree to this position. David then opened his briefcase and placed his brief on the table. Jokingly, I asked him if we were going to negotiate. He laughed and said that as we were friends, he wanted to read me the relevant portion on the triggering mechanism. I had no reason to doubt him in any case. All that was left to do was confirm the date for the talks.

When the full negotiations commenced later that month in Wellington, our respective negotiating teams were spared the agony of talking both to, and at, each other for the three days that were set aside for the talks. Instead, we reached an agreement within 15 minutes following a short debate on the ills of Flight Uplift and Discharge or 6th Freedom rights. This was just the Kiwis having a bit of a dig at SIA, which was taken in good spirit by all.

We had started off with total pessimism but sheer persistence and meetings with senior civil servants, the Transport Minister and a defiant union, with a measure of drama thrown in on my part, finally paid off and enabled us to get a decent agreement for SIA and overall, a satisfactory enhancement of the bilateral Air Services Agreement between Singapore and New Zealand.

Re-Examining the Human Rights Issue in ASEAN

by Barry Desker

On 18 June 2020, the Association of Southeast Asian Nations (ASEAN) Parliamentarians for Human Rights (APHR) issued a report "*In Singapore, an Already Unfair Vote Undermined by COVID-19*". The report argued that the lack of independent oversight, the group representation constituency system, strict media restrictions and the short campaigning period created insurmountable difficulties for opposition candidates. The report also claimed that the COVID-19 pandemic and electoral measures introduced in the light of the pandemic had failed "to ensure a fair campaigning process during the pandemic, or protect the voting rights for specific groups, particularly the sick and overseas voters". The report re-hashed well-trodden ground in criticising the Singapore government's approach to periodic general elections and did not address the increasing participation of Singaporeans in domestic politics despite the restrictions. The drafters of the report also appeared to have failed to recognise that the "hundreds of new daily coronavirus cases" were foreign workers living in dormitories without the right to participate in the elections. This report highlights the highly contextual nature of human rights in Singapore and ASEAN.

Human Rights and the ASEAN Charter

Nevertheless, the emergence of APHR and civil society organisations as actors within ASEAN frameworks is one significant development arising from the adoption of the ASEAN Charter in Singapore in November 2007. In a break with ASEAN's earlier focus on sovereignty and previously steadfast claims of non-intervention and non-interference in the internal affairs of member states, one of the principles of the Charter explicitly called on member states to act in "respect for fundamental freedoms, the promotion and protection of human rights, and the promotion of social justice".

The Charter's reference to the establishment of an ASEAN human rights body was the basis for the establishment of the ASEAN Inter-Governmental Commission on Human Rights (AICHR) at the 15th ASEAN Summit in Cha-am, Hua Hin, Thailand, in October 2009. The initial group of AICHR representatives prepared the ASEAN Human Rights Declaration adopted at the ASEAN Summit in Phnom Penh in November 2012. The Declaration included General Principles as well as provisions on civil and political rights, economic and cultural rights, together with sections on the right to development and the right to peace. This did not satisfy some Western observers who felt that the Declaration fell short of existing human rights standards.

From a Singapore standpoint, the Declaration reflected a balance between the varying strands of ASEAN opinion. The late Richard Magnus, a retired Chief District Judge, served as Singapore's first AICHR representative from 2009 to 2012 and played an active role in the drafting of the Declaration. In November 2012, Magnus was succeeded by Chan Heng Chee, who had served as Ambassador to the United States from 1996 to 2012.

AICHR Raises the Human Rights Profile within ASEAN

Although the ASEAN foreign ministers had reached a consensus on the inter-governmental nature of the Commission, several member states appointed human rights activists involved in civil society and non-governmental organisations (NGOs) as their nominees. These representatives sought a role in

AICHR for NGOs active in human rights issues, the participation of civil society representatives in AICHR-organised workshops and seminars, and outreach by AICHR to the wider international human rights community. They also pushed for formal recognition of agreed NGOs within the ASEAN framework. When I succeeded Chan Heng Chee in January 2016, Thailand's representative Dr. Seree Nonthasoot, an academic with an international law background, was re-appointed for a second term, while Malaysia nominated Edmund Bon, a human rights lawyer, and Indonesia appointed Dr. Dinna Wisnu, an academic and civil society activist. The other ASEAN states selected serving or recently retired officials. I served as the Chair of AICHR in 2018, before completing my three-year term.

The divergence within ASEAN on the approach to NGOs, also frequently described as civil society organisations (CSOs), shaped individual states' policy preferences on issues such as responses to letters and communications from civil society, the participation of civil society observers in AICHR meetings and outreach by AICHR to the wider international human rights community. Although some countries had wanted a mechanism to deal with complaints on human rights violations during the drafting of AICHR's terms of reference (TOR), there was no consensus, and the issue was excluded to enable adoption of the TOR. Among issues raised at "off the record" AICHR retreats was the disappearance of the prominent Laotian activist Sombath Somphone and the massive refugee crisis arising from the eviction of Rohingyas from the Rakhine state in Myanmar. While initially one-way briefings without any exchange of views proposed, eventually the AICHR representatives received such briefings in informal "off the record" sessions, which allowed them to engage the representative of the concerned member state. While some representatives with activist backgrounds felt that AICHR should move from the promotion of human rights to active protection of human rights, there was strong resistance particularly from Myanmar, Laos, Vietnam and Cambodia.

Among AICHR's external partners, the European Union was the most active in sponsoring AICHR workshops, seminars and public events, while a range of countries and international organisations also supported AICHR's activities, including the United States, Australia, Japan, South Korea and various United Nations (UN) agencies. This led to internal

AICHR debates as there was a concern that AICHR's agenda would be shaped by the keen interest of the EU and other Western powers in promoting individual civil and political rights, and the participation of CSOs, especially on issues such as the death penalty, LGBT rights, preventive detention and the rights of migrant workers on which there were divergent positions among the ASEAN members. The role of AICHR's external partners and the funding of AICHR activities was the subject of close attention by AICHR representatives. Consequently, AICHR reviews of concept papers for planned activities developed into a substantive aspect of AICHR's work programme. The representatives attempted to ensure that AICHR remained in the driving seat determining its own agenda instead of having its activities shaped by its external partners, who were often the major source of funding.

Since 2017, AICHR has also been meeting annually with CSOs, enjoying a consultative relationship with AICHR. Thirty CSOs have been accredited. A wide range of topics has been covered, including dialogues on the rights of women, children and persons with disabilities as well as discussions on issues such as trafficking in persons, the right to education, business and human rights and environmental protection. I therefore encouraged Singapore CSOs to seek accreditation with AICHR. The Singapore Council of Women's Organisations was accredited in 2015 while MARUAH (Working Group for an ASEAN Human Rights Mechanism, Singapore) and the Movement for the Intellectually Disabled of Singapore (MINDS) were accredited by AICHR during my term.

I also organised roundtable discussions with Singapore CSOs as well as met with the leaders of individual CSOs. Through this process, I engaged a wide range of Singapore CSOs including the AICHR-accredited CSOs as well as CSOs dealing with subjects such as the death penalty, the environment, LGBT rights, migrant workers, corporate social responsibility as well as the rights of women, children and persons with disabilities. The range of issues advanced by CSOs in Singapore reflected the emergence of a post-materialist society in Singapore. While an earlier generation of Singaporeans focused on socio-economic upliftment, younger Singaporeans are increasingly drawn to quality-of-life issues. My approach was to have an exchange of views, even on issues on which the government had a well-established position. The aim was to provide an opportunity for CSOs to raise issues of their concern, which could be conveyed to the relevant ministries, as representatives of the relevant ministries were invited to these meetings. The feedback from the participants was that while some of the CSOs were not satisfied with my responses, which reflected the position of the government, they recognised that this process created a channel of contact with policymaking institutions in Singapore.

Institutional Development of AICHR

As AICHR was moving into areas beyond the remit of foreign ministries, the representatives agreed that AICHR should engage with the Senior Officials Meeting on Social Welfare and Development (SOMSWD) and the Senior Economic Officials Meetings (SEOM), besides the ASEAN Senior Officials Meeting (ASEAN SOM) composed of foreign ministry officials. At these meetings, issues such as the mainstreaming of the rights of persons with disabilities and the rights of women and children were taken up. It also led to the inclusion of participants from the relevant ministries in AICHR's consideration of issues such as its consultations on corporate social responsibility, the right to safe drinking water and sanitation and the right to food. Interactions with SEOM took longer to materialise as the ASEAN economic officials have traditionally seen themselves as reporting directly to the ASEAN economic ministers and did not recognise the convening role of the foreign ministry-led ASEAN Foreign Ministers Meetings (AMM). From a Singapore perspective, greater collaboration among ASEAN sectoral bodies was sought so that a silo mentality within government agencies could be avoided. I therefore played an active role in encouraging these initiatives.

While AICHR is the overarching ASEAN human rights institution, institutional independence of the meetings of the ASEAN ministers of social welfare and development led to the establishment of another three institutions: the ASEAN Commission on the Promotion and Protection of the Rights of Women and Children (ACWC), the ASEAN Committee on Women (ACW) and the ASEAN Committee on the Implementation of the ASEAN Declaration on the Protection and Promotion of the Rights of Migrant Workers (ACMW). To overcome the risk of overlapping initiatives, AICHR and SOMSWD agreed to collaborate closely on issues relating to human rights. This development during my AICHR term helped to reduce the competition between these ASEAN bodies and promoted cooperation among officials and CSOs involved in these areas.

ASEAN and International Human Rights Conventions

The establishment of AICHR led to informal pressures to ratify or accede to the nine core UN human rights instruments as the accession record of member states is discussed at AICHR meetings. As all UN member states also have to present a report every four and a half years to the Universal Periodic Review (UPR) of the UN Human Rights Council and answer questions from UN members, there has been an upward trend in the ratification or accession to these conventions.

Singapore is party to the Convention on the Elimination of All Forms of Discrimination Against Women (CEDAW), the Convention on the Rights of the Child (CRC), the Convention on the Rights of Persons with Disabilities (CRPD) and the Convention on the Elimination of All Forms of Racial Discrimination (ICERD). As a state with communitarian values, it is ironic that Singapore has not yet acceded to the International Covenant on Economic, Social and Cultural Rights (ICESCR). This Covenant was a product of the Cold War. The Soviet bloc and non-aligned states sought to shift attention away from the Western focus on individual and personal rights in the International Covenant on the Civil and Political Rights (ICCPR) by emphasising the rights of the community, as reflected in the ICESCR. At that time, in the 1970s and 1980s, Singapore emphasised the need for a balanced approach to human rights which required a recognition that individual rights needed to be weighed against social obligations and the interests of the community.

One aspect of human rights that has attracted attention recently in Singapore has been the management of foreign worker dormitories and the need to meet the basic needs of foreign workers in Singapore. Singapore human rights activists have raised this issue previously without any impact in Singapore. With the epidemic of COVID-19 infections in the dormitories, there is now greater awareness of how this can adversely impact Singapore society. The government has moved decisively to improve conditions for workers living in these dormitories, especially as it is now recognised that other infections can easily spread in the cramped conditions.

Singapore activists drew attention to Malaysia's handling of human rights issues, which they viewed positively. Despite Malaysia taking a high profile on this subject during the tenure of the Pakatan Harapan coalition, especially on the rights of Palestinians and Rohingya refugees, it has moved even more slowly on accession to UN Human Rights Conventions. With at least 2.2 million documented foreign workers and another 3 to 4 million undocumented illegal workers, Malaysia, like Singapore, is unlikely to accede to the International Convention on the Protection of the Rights of All Migrant Workers and Members of Their Families (ICRMW), an issue raised within the AICHR by the representatives of Indonesia and the Philippines, which are Malaysia's leading sources of migrant workers. A second example is Malaysia's lack of action on the Convention on the Elimination of All Forms of Racial Discrimination (ICERD). In May 2018, when the Pakatan Harapan coalition took over from the Barisan Nasional coalition led by Najib Razak after its stunning election victory, human rights activists within the government pushed for early accession to the ICERD. Strong counter-vailing domestic pressure from Malays concerned that accession to ICERD would undermine Malay special rights resulted in the Cabinet reversing its decision. The Malaysian government did not proceed with its campaign pledge to accede to ICERD, and another coalition government is unlikely to change this decision.

However, accession to UN Conventions does not necessarily mean that states uphold their commitments. Cambodia, for example, has acceded to all the nine core instruments except for the ICRMW but it continues to be in the news for forced disappearances, allegations of torture and as a haven for child prostitution and child pornography. While Thailand has played an active role in widening and deepening coverage of human rights issues in AICHR, severe penalties for *lèse majesté* offences and disappearances of junta critics remain the practice in Bangkok. The same is true of Indonesia, which has witnessed a decline in the protection of religious minorities including Shia, Ahmadiyya and Christians in the post-Suharto era as well as the torture, extra-judicial killings and forced disappearances of West Papuan dissidents. Similarly, while the Philippines has been a leading voice on civil and political rights issues in AICHR and the UN, there has been a sharp upward trend in summary executions of alleged drug dealers and criminals in the country.

The Eagle Meets the Panda

The debate within ASEAN on human rights issues was also influenced by developments in the international geo-political environment. With the fall of the Berlin Wall in 1989 and the collapse of the Soviet Union, the United States was the sole superpower and the European Union expanded significantly into the former Soviet bloc in Eastern Europe. Western values were in the ascendancy. This was reflected in the fall of military-led governments such as the Suharto administration in Indonesia, greater democratisation in Taiwan and South Korea, "colour revolutions" in Europe and the enunciation of doctrines such as the Responsibility to Protect, which justified the right of humanitarian intervention, as well as the establishment of the International Criminal Court. This approach emphasised the political and civil rights of the individual, which were deemed to be universal values, and led to the rise of civil society groups influenced by these doctrines. The problem was that this resulted in a culture-bound definition of human rights, which was associated with the promotion of Western values and Western ideals highlighting the personal rights and interests of the individual. This was the context in which the framers of AICHR pursued their effort to implement the Phnom Penh Declaration and explained the criticisms of Western human rights groups of AICHR processes and ASEAN's commitment to universal human rights.

At the same time, the 1980s and 1990s was also the era which witnessed the dramatic economic emergence of China, India and states in East Asia. No one can argue today that the Chinese government fails to meet the basic needs of its citizens or that the lives of ordinary Chinese people have not improved immeasurably compared to 40 years ago. The Chinese leadership's focus is on the broader interests of Chinese society through economic development, social cohesion and political stability. The current generation of Chinese nationals appears strongly supportive of their political leadership and its efforts to shape the domestic and global environment. Similarly, Japan has a strong sense of Japanese identity and its recovery from the collapse at the end of the Second World War has been attributed to the social solidarity and unity of purpose of the Japanese people. Group and community interests take precedence over the preferences of the individual. Some observers have identified this as the "secret" of Japan's low incidence of COVID-19 infections.

In this context, the current COVID-19 pandemic has raised pertinent questions about the balance between individual rights and community interests. Governments have been forced to restrict the activities of their citizens and to utilise technology for contact tracing. They have also imposed travel restrictions, required the use of masks in public places and placed limits on personal freedom through the imposition of lockdowns. The United States faced major difficulties in imposing these restrictions, resulting in it having the worst pandemic outbreak globally. China, by contrast, which was the original source of the COVID-19 pandemic, effectively managed the outbreak by taking decisive action, after initially failing to control its spread.

These developments will influence states in the East Asian region. My assessment is that the communitarian instincts of governments in East Asia will lead to a growing questioning of the current dominant international perspectives in the field of human rights. The measured approach taken by AICHR is likely to be closer to the new norm in the years ahead as the global balance shifts away from unipolar dominance by the United States.

It is a reminder that the adoption of the Universal Declaration of Human Rights by the UN in 1948 was the first time that human rights featured on the global multilateral institutional agenda. At that time, the Declaration was perceived as a multi-faceted doctrine capable of divergent interpretations compared to the current interpretation which emphasises individual and personal rights. The Declaration was both pluralistic and flexible and did not impose a single ideological view on signatory states, allowing even the Soviet Union and its new client states in Eastern Europe to support the Declaration. With the rise of China, and a renewed confidence among states in East Asia as well as India, there will be a growing challenge to Western doctrines of human rights emphasising personal rights of the individual. Winning support for a regional and global human rights agenda in the years ahead will require proponents to push for an awareness of individual civil and political rights as well as recognition of the social, cultural and economic rights of the community.

My Journey as a Peacemaker

by Tommy Koh

One of my life-long aspirations is peace: peace in the family, peace in the country and peace in the world. It is my good fortune to have been asked to make peace in all three domains.

Peace in the Family

Many years ago, the patriarch of a very wealthy family passed away. He left his wealth to his three children. Two of his children lived in Singapore. The third lived in Malaysia. There was a difference of opinion between the children about the future of the father's company. The child in Malaysia wanted to dissolve the company. The two in Singapore wanted to keep the company. The family asked me to be the mediator.

I flew to Kuala Lumpur to see the child who lived there. He was adamant that his father's company be dissolved and for the proceeds to be equally divided among the three siblings. I asked him whether he would consider selling his share to his siblings, he said no. I was therefore not successful in my mediation. The lesson learnt is that when trust has been lost and goodwill has been replaced by ill will, no compromise is possible.

Peace in the Country

Singapore has an excellent Mediation Centre. I am on the panel of mediators. One day, the centre informed me that my services were required. A civil servant had been dismissed by one of our ministries. She felt that she had been wrongfully dismissed. She had sued the government in the High Court. The judge advised her to try the mediation option first. She told the Mediation Centre that she would agree to refer her case to mediation provided that I agree to be the mediator. I did not know her. As a civil servant, I had to get the permission of the Head of the Civil Service to serve as mediator because the defendant was the government. Permission was granted.

I had to study several bags of documents which the complainant had submitted. One of the documents contained a legal opinion given to her by one of our ministers, when he was in the private sector. He had advised her that she had a good case. I then conducted an oral proceeding to hear both sides. The government was represented by a very able lawyer from the Attorney-General's Chambers. I drew her attention to the legal opinion. As a compromise, I suggested that, without admitting liability, the government should pay the complainant X number of months of salary. The suggestion was accepted by the complainant and, surprisingly, rejected by the government.

Peaceful Settlement of Trade Disputes

In 1996, the World Trade Organization (WTO) held its first Ministerial Meeting in Singapore. I was a member of the Singapore delegation, led by our then Minister for Trade and Industry, Mr. Yeo Cheow Tong. My job was to help the Minister in chairing the meetings and negotiations. As a result, I got to know the late WTO Director-General, Dr. Renato Ruggiero, and his senior colleagues. In the following four years, I was asked to serve on three dispute panels, twice as Chairman.

In 1998, the WTO informed me that New Zealand and the United States (US) had brought a complaint against Canada. The three countries had requested that I chair the dispute panel consisting of three members. The Singapore government advised me to accept because of our strong support for the WTO and because we believe in the peaceful settlement of disputes.

The complaint by New Zealand and the US was that, contrary to WTO law, Canada was providing subsidies on dairy products through its national and provincial pricing mechanisms for milk and other dairy products. The Dispute Panel unanimously found in favour of New Zealand and the US, and we were upheld on appeal.

In the year 2000, I was again informed by the WTO that Australia, New Zealand and the US had nominated me to chair a Dispute Panel, to consider a dispute brought by Australia and New Zealand against the US. The issue was whether the US law on safeguards was consistent with the WTO law. The panel unanimously found that the US law was not consistent with the WTO law and we were upheld on appeal.

The compulsory dispute settlement system of the WTO is a precious achievement. It should be protected against those who are trying to undermine it.

Making Peace Between Russia and its Baltic Neighbours

In 1993, the late United Nations (UN) Secretary-General Dr. Boutros Boutros-Ghali appointed me as his Special Envoy to make peace between Russia, on the one hand, and Estonia, Latvia and Lithuania on the other. During the Cold War, the three countries had been incorporated, against their will, into the Soviet Union. With the end of the Cold War, all three countries became independent.

In 1993, there were between 5,000 and 6,000 Russian troops in Estonia. There were also about 50,000 Russian veterans and retirees living in Estonia. In 1993, there were about 18,000 Russian troops in Latvia. There were about 20,000 Russian veterans and retirees living in Latvia. In addition, there were a Russian naval base, an anti-ballistic missile early warning system and another facility of disputed function in Latvia.

Diplomats from Russia and the three Baltic countries were unable to agree on a timetable for the withdrawal of the Russian troops and the closing of the Russian facilities. The UN Secretary-General was asked by a UN General Assembly resolution to use his good offices. He, in turn, appointed me to do the job.

I accepted the job with great reluctance as I had never been to the four countries. I went first to the UN to be briefed. I then proceeded to Moscow to meet the Russian Vice Foreign Minister and his three negotiators. I then went to visit Lithuania, Latvia and Estonia. I then went back to Moscow. As a result of the help by the then US Ambassador in Moscow, Tom Pickering, I was able to meet with a member of the personal staff of President Boris Yeltsin in the Kremlin. Neither the UN nor the Singapore Embassy was able to get me such an appointment. This was an important meeting as it gave me an opportunity to seek the support of President Yeltsin directly for my mission.

I then returned to New York to write my report to the Secretary-General. In my report, I proposed a timetable for the withdrawal of the Russian troops from Estonia and Latvia. I also proposed a timetable for closing down the Russian facilities in Latvia. I was very gratified that my proposals were accepted by the four countries. In Estonia and Latvia, I had advised the two governments to treat their Russian minorities with kindness. I warned them that if they did not do so, they would be loyal to Russia and not to their adopted countries.

Conclusion

Peace is precious. It is one of the most fervent wishes of people everywhere and throughout history. I am grateful that I have been able to make a very small contribution to peace in the world.

POSTSCRIPT: WHAT MAKES FOREIGN POLICY WORK BEYOND THE HANDSHAKE

A Career in Diplomacy

by A. Selverajah

My career in diplomacy spanned 40 years with postings in Asia, Europe and America. When I joined the Ministry of Foreign Affairs (MFA) in 1979, I did not think that I would stay so long. Looking in from the outside, the work of diplomats appears to be glamorous and prestigious. As representatives of your country, diplomats are expected to dress well, carry themselves with dignity and be given privileges and immunities in their countries of posting to help them do their job well. However, behind it is a lot of hard work, long hours, travels and disruptions to yourself and your family caused by alternating between home and overseas postings. A diplomat's work involves dealing with an unpredictable international environment both when he is home and at overseas postings. So, it is in a sense a 24/7 job.

As a diplomat, the main satisfaction that you derive is the little contribution you are making to advance Singapore's national interests. When you are at home, you work on formulating foreign policy. In postings, you strive to advance Singapore's political, economic and strategic interests by working with your host government to build a mutually beneficial win–win partnership that will broaden and deepen the relationship between Singapore and your host country. Small countries have no intrinsic value in the international system, and we must take the world as it is, and not what we would like it to be. Thus, Singapore has to constantly make itself relevant to the world, forge friendships with as many countries as possible and value-add where we can to the issues confronting the international system. This is the essence of Singapore's proactive diplomacy. It can only be achieved by a political leadership that takes a long-term view and can see beyond the curve to navigate the international system, supported by dedicated, knowledgeable and skilled diplomats.

Bangkok

I served in six countries in my 40-year career in the diplomatic service. And in every country, the challenges and opportunities for advancing Singapore's foreign policy interests were different. When I first went to Bangkok as First Secretary and then as Counsellor, we were preoccupied with the Cambodian issue. The Vietnamese had occupied Cambodia, arguing that their objective was to rid the country of the Khmer Rouge. Singapore, together with our other Association of Southeast Asian Nations (ASEAN) partners, opposed Vietnam's occupation; at stake was the breach of a fundamental principle of the United Nations (UN) Charter that no country has the right to violate the territorial integrity of another country. If we had condoned this, it would have set a bad precedent, especially for the survival of small countries like Singapore. We worked with Thailand, a frontline state, as it was critical to prevent Thailand and other non-Communist states of Southeast Asia from falling to Communism.

My colleagues and I at the Embassy had the responsibility to keep Singapore updated on Thailand's thinking and views, both on the diplomatic front and the efforts by the Khmer Rouge and the Non-Communist Resistance (NCR) on the ground against the Vietnamese. We also needed to know what China and Thailand were discussing as China supported the Khmer Rouge and ASEAN the NCR, and we were therefore engaged in a common mission of denying Vietnam a fait accompli in Cambodia. In 1988, when the new Thai Prime Minister (PM), the late Chatichai Choonhavan, suddenly changed policy by reaching out to the Vietnamese-installed Cambodian government without consulting the Thai Foreign Ministry and ASEAN, it changed the dynamics of the Cambodian issue. This, in turn, required Singapore to reevaluate its own position. As a political officer at our Embassy, it was part of my responsibility to talk to Thai government officials, diplomatic, military, media and other contacts in Bangkok and file timely and analytical reports to MFA Headquarters (HQ). These reports helped Singapore to formulate the right policies as the issue evolved, both in terms of our support on the ground for the NCR and our diplomatic campaign at the UN.

Years later, when former Thai PM Prem Tinsulanonda passed away and PM Lee Hsien Loong in his condolence message recalled Prem's contribution to holding the line against the Vietnamese occupation of Cambodia, the Vietnamese and Cambodians expressed unhappiness with PM's comments. But what was more surprising was that some Singaporeans were asking why we were so insensitive and felt the need to bring up old issues. These Singaporeans had failed to realise that what was at stake was a violation of a fundamental principle of the UN Charter which, if allowed to be ignored with impunity, would be particularly dangerous for small countries like Singapore. It was for this reason that Singapore had invested 12 years in the diplomatic effort worldwide and the resistance on the ground to deny the Vietnamese a fait accompli in Cambodia.

After my Bangkok posting, I returned to MFA HQ and served as a Deputy Director and later as a Director. In HQ, the nature of the work is different from that of a posting. Here you are a recipient of the various reports coming from the missions reporting to your Directorate and you are required to process these reports, identify key trends and send them onto senior management, supervise the writing of briefing papers for visits to and from Singapore, accompany our political leaders on visits and undertake a range of duties that concern promoting the relationship between Singapore and the countries under your charge. As MFA HQ serves as the hub for the network of Singapore's overseas missions and with the time differences between Singapore and its various missions, you spend long hours in the office preparing policy papers, recommendations and reports for visits to and from Singapore for our political leaders. Later, I was posted to Washington, D.C. as Deputy Chief of Mission (DCM) in February 1994. When I called to say farewell to my Permanent Secretary, Mr. Kishore Mahbubani, he told me that I "should hit the ground running on APEC" as we had just returned from a successful Asia-Pacific

Economic Cooperation (APEC) Summit in Blake Island, United States (US), in December 1993.

Washington, D.C.

However, I arrived in Washington right in the middle of the Michael Fay case. It then dawned on me that in MFA, you can never exactly predict how your posting would turn out. Thus, beyond being a 24/7 Ministry, we also had to be always prepared to deal with unpredictable developments. So as I was doing my two-week overlap with Ong Keng Yong (now an Ambassador-at-Large at MFA and Deputy Chairman of RSIS) who kindly took me around and introduced me to many useful contacts, we heard that Israeli Radio had reported that a Jewish boy was caught spray-painting cars in Singapore which was considered vandalism and carried a mandatory caning penalty. I did not even have time to settle down with my wife and two young children, having joined me three weeks later. For the next three months, my colleagues at the Embassy and I were dealing primarily with the Michael Fay case. We were not helped by the fact that there is a 12-hour time difference between Singapore and Washington, D.C., and that meant we had to work until 11 pm or midnight most days.

Then President Bill Clinton and his administration pressured us to do away with the caning sentence, even raising questions about whether Fay had been given a fair trial. Initially the American public was supportive of Singapore because they felt that Singapore had the right to enforce its own laws and the US might be better off having strict laws to deal with the breakdown of law and order in some of their inner cities. But the US liberal media supported the Clinton Administration and painted the caning punishment as barbaric and medieval, which caused American public opinion to shift against us. But the media's call to American businesses to pull out of Singapore and appeals to Congress went largely unheeded. Fortunately, the Embassy was able to handle the crisis as we had an experienced Ambassador, the late Mr. S. R. Nathan, who later became the President of Singapore, and dedicated colleagues Lim Thuan Kuan, who became Ambassador to ASEAN, India and is currently High Commissioner to the UK, First Secretary Ng Teck Hean, who became Ambassador to Vietnam and is now a Deputy Secretary in MFA and Chin Hock Seng, who later became Chief of Protocol in MFA. We had to keep our cool in the face of the negative media publicity and the thousands of phone calls we received from the American public, including some threatening ones.

As I reflected on this episode, it told me about the reality that small countries must face in international relations. Singapore has always viewed the US positively, treated it as a good friend and has always been a strong advocate for a continued US presence in the Asia-Pacific. The US was also a country where the rule of law was applied without fear or favour. Yet the US Administration chose to pressurise Singapore on a law-and-order issue, questioning its sovereign right to enforce its laws. The US must have known that yielding to US pressure to do away with the caning sentence completely would have made Singapore lose all credibility in the eyes of the international community and made it appear as a client state of the US. The Singapore government, in its wisdom, decided to give some weight to President Clinton's appeal. It still enforced the caning sentence decided by the judiciary but reduced the number of strokes from six to four. The episode also made me wonder whether as a small country, friendship counted for anything and whether the Clinton Administration would have put similar pressure on us had we been a bigger country. This is one of the realities that Singapore has to reckon with in the conduct of its foreign policy.

Ambassador in Brussels

My subsequent postings were as Ambassador in Brussels with accreditation to the European Union (EU), the Netherlands, Luxembourg and Vatican. As a small country, Singapore had to make itself relevant to the world and our ambassadors, besides reporting on political and economic developments in their host country, also had to look out for opportunities to broaden and deepen the relationship between Singapore and the countries to which they are accredited. Nine months after my arrival in Brussels, then PM Goh Chok Tong made an official visit to the EU in June 2000. As a country where trade is our lifeline and the total amount of trade that we conduct is three times the size of our gross domestic product, Singapore was concerned about the lack of progress on the Doha Round of the World Trade Organization (WTO) and had begun to negotiate bilateral and regional free trade agreements (FTAs) that were WTO-plus, which meant that they went beyond what was in the Doha Round agenda. Singapore believed that such FTAs were necessary to keep up the momentum for a rules-based free and fair multilateral trading system.

In Brussels, PM Goh proposed an EU–Singapore FTA to then EU President Romano Prodi. Prodi was supportive. However, the new Directorate General for Trade at the European Commission Pascal Lamy wanted to focus on the WTO and was not enthusiastic about the EU concluding any new bilateral or regional FTAs. Nevertheless, my colleagues at the Mission and I proceeded to lobby Lamy and the Permanent Representatives of the EU in Brussels for an early start to negotiate the EU–Singapore FTA. Since Singapore saw it in its interest to negotiate the FTA, we actively lobbied the European Commission. The EU–Singapore FTA was finally concluded 19 years later in 2019. Had I known in 2000 that it would take so long to conclude this FTA, I wonder if my Embassy colleagues and I would have worked with the same enthusiasm and intensity from 2000 to 2003, when I was posted from Brussels to Berlin. But what it shows is that in diplomacy, you sometimes have to sow the seeds and work hard at it, even though the initiative might bear fruit only many years later.

Ambassador to the Holy See

When I was appointed as Ambassador to the Holy See, Singapore had a Third Country Technical Cooperation Programme (TCTP) with the Vatican under which we jointly funded the teaching of the English language to Laotians and Cambodians in their respective countries. We were indeed one of a few countries with which the Vatican had a technical cooperation programme.

During a visit to the Vatican Museum in Rome, I was impressed with its collection of invaluable artifacts. Since Singapore had a sizeable Catholic community, I proposed to our Asian Civilisations Museum to work with the Vatican Museum to bring and showcase some of these artifacts in Singapore. At first the Vatican Museum was reluctant, as they were concerned about the transport and security of these artefacts.

However, after a few meetings, I was able to persuade the then Vatican Secretary of State for International Relations, Archbishop Jean Louis Tauran, to accept our proposal. The Asian Civilisations Museum then identified some artefacts showcasing how Catholicism was brought to Southeast Asia by St. Francis Xavier. The artefacts were then sent to Singapore and displayed at an exhibition entitled "The Journey of Faith" for six months, which was well received and attracted many visitors.

Ambassador in Berlin

From Brussels, I went as Ambassador to Germany in 2003 and stayed there until 2008. There I realised that the job of an ambassador encompasses advancing all aspects of Singapore's interests in the host country, which can be political, economic, security, cultural and so on. We had no major political issues with Germany, but we had a strong interest in attracting German companies, both the big multinational corporations (MNCs) and German small and medium-sized enterprises (SMEs) to Singapore. I recognised that given our interests, one important part of my job as ambassador would be to open doors for the Economic Development Board (EDB) officers in Germany to gain access to the chief executive officers and board members of the German MNCs and SMEs. To achieve this, I visited all the German states with EDB officers, who were well-prepared and made professional presentations at the meetings which impressed our German interlocutors. Similarly, I attended the trade fairs at the German Messe (Exhibition Halls) to show the flag when Singapore companies showcased their products. The job of an ambassador and how you contribute on the ground is ultimately what you make of it without having to always wait for instructions from MFA HQ.

Ambassador in Manila

In 2008, I was cross posted from Berlin as Ambassador to the Philippines. I recognised that with the Philippines, besides our bilateral relations, we also had the ASEAN aspect to deal with. So, one of my tasks was to see how we could work with the Philippines to advance our common interests in ASEAN. To commemorate the 40th anniversary of Singapore–Philippine relations, I tried to bring a pair of Philippine eagles to our Jurong Bird Park, but we could not agree to the Philippines' terms in the memorandum of understanding to be concluded by our Wildlife Reserve and the Philippine authorities. However, I was gratified to read that the eagles finally arrived in Singapore 10 years later for the 50th anniversary of Singapore–Philippine diplomatic relations in 2019. Another illustration of the fact that you sometimes sow the seeds and the fruits come much later after you have left the post. But that should not deter you from sowing the seeds.

Ambassador in Ankara

My final posting was as the first resident Ambassador of Singapore to Turkey. Thanks to the efforts of my predecessor, Non-Resident Ambassador Chandra Das, we had signed a Declaration on a Strategic Partnership with Turkey and a Turkey–Singapore FTA. I was hoping to use these platforms to build on the work of my predecessor. But again, as I stated earlier, you cannot predict what will happen at a posting. Before I left for Ankara, I was told that it was a quiet and uneventful place as the hub of activity in Turkey was Istanbul. But two months after I arrived in Ankara, a suicide bomber detonated himself at the train station in Ankara. ISIS in neighbouring Syria was at its height. I heard the explosions of suicide and car bombs in Ankara. In addition, I was in my apartment in a high-rise building on 15 October 2016 when there was a failed coup attempt and the coup plotters had bombed the Turkish Parliament, Police Headquarters and the Turkish Radio and Television station.

There were also other terrorist attacks in Istanbul and the Istanbul airport. The Russian Ambassador in Ankara was tragically assassinated by a Gulenist, a member of the group that had staged the failed coup. A climate of psychological fear and uncertainty pervaded Ankara and other parts of Turkey for 18 months between July 2015 and January 2017. It was in this atmosphere that my colleagues and I at the Embassy had to operate with concern for our safety, that of our families and that of our locally recruited staff. Little did I expect any of this when I started my posting. Another illustration of how the unexpected can confront you in a posting in any form from a diplomatic crisis like Michael Fay to serious security concerns over terrorist activities in Turkey. All that said, the 40-year journey has been one eventful ride and as in any other job, if you do it with all the passion that you can muster, it has its rewards.

Postscript

After retirement, ambassadors can continue to contribute to MFA in important ways. Ours is a small, but well-regarded Foreign Service and it would be a waste if the cumulative knowledge and experiences, together with the skills and values acquired by one generation of Foreign Service officers (FSOs), are not passed on to the next generation. Each generation of FSOs ought to take on the responsibility to help build up the next generation of FSOs. I realised the value of this when I was the Dean of the Diplomatic Academy, and we organised fireside chats, lectures and panel discussions for courses on Southeast Asia, the US, China and the Middle East by tapping on the experiences and knowledge of older FSOs. Younger FSOs will benefit from the skills and values that older FSOs can pass on to them; sound advice that they cannot obtain merely by reading the briefs, submissions and notes of conversation.

I am grateful to MFA for appointing me, after my retirement, as a senior fellow in the MFA Diplomatic Academy and as a Non-Resident Ambassador to the Federal Democratic Republic of Ethiopia and the African Union, in which capacities I hope to continue to make a modest contribution to the Ministry.